Praise for the Biblical Studies series

" ... Grounded, thorough, well-supported and able to be understood."

"... Solid refutations for common arguments against the validity of Scripture ... "

" ... Pleasantly surprised to find a few new concepts and validations that I had not come across before."

Biblical Studies Teacher Edition
Part One: Old Testament

by

Michael J. and Mary C. Findley

Findley Family Video Publications

Second Edition

Biblical Studies Teacher Edition Part One: Old Testament 2nd Edition

Findley Family Video Publications

"Speaking the truth in love."

Scripture references are as follows: The Bible: The king James Version, public domain. RV (English Revised Version), also public domain. (Please see the Authors' Note within the doctrinal study materials on Evans' language, Style and Content for information concerning this translation.)

Table of Contents

Introduction to this Compilation of Bible Study Materials

History of the Bible Part One: Authority, Old Testament and Translations

Part One Review Questions

Bible Doctrines Review Questions

based on The Great Doctrines of the Bible by Rev. William Evans

Ruth (from The Slow of Heart Children's Bible Study Series)

Ruth Commentary by the Anything Box Characters

Ruth Review Questions

Proverbs Review Questions

Major Prophets Background Study

Major Prophets Review Questions

Jonah (from The Slow of Heart Children's Bible Study Series)

Jonah Commentary by the Anything Box Characters

Jonah Review Questions

Other Products from Findley Family Video

Introduction to This Compilation of Biblical Study Materials

This collection of biblical studies represents years of teaching to various age groups. Many are correlated with videos available free on YouTube at http://www.youtube.com/user/ffvp5657. Links to specific videos appear in the section they are to be used with. Study questions are included with each section.

Short, objective study questions follow each title's reading material. The Teacher Edition contains the complete text of the student book plus any notes to the teacher. Also included in the Teacher Edition are optional and supplementary questions. These include essays, research projects, or any questions requiring longer answers, which can be assigned at the discretion of the teacher.

Note to Teacher: Students will need to write answers in a separate file or on a sheet of paper.

History of the Bible Part One:
Authority, Old Testament and Translations

Preservation of the Word through the Old Testament Period Including Topical Manuscript Studies

The Law, the Prophets, and the Writings
Ugaritic and Ancient Hebrew
The Septuagint
The Masoretic Text
The Syriac Peshitta
The Dead Sea Scrolls

Creation Museum's Prophets of the Old Testament exhibit, Isaiah. Photo released into the Public Domain by the photographer.

History of the Bible Part One: Old Testament

Preservation of the Word through the Old Testament Period

Preservation of the Word through the Old Testament Period

Even if some parts of the Bible were handed down through oral transmission, they are still accurate. Incredibly, some people who dare to call themselves "scholars" claim that Hebrews of the Kingdom period did not have a written language. The only reason for making this outrageous claim is to manufacture doubt about the reliability of the Old Testament. They can claim it had to be written later, undermining the possibility of correct chronology and accuracy of prophecies.

A terra cotta tablet list of gods of Ugarit was excavated at Ras Shamra. It is in the Louvre, Paris, France.

(Ugarit is written in cuneiform but is almost identical to ancient Hebrew and unlike other cuneiform languages. See Appendix for more information.)

Not even the discovery of actual kingdom period written Hebrew could convince some people. The Hebrew alphabet from the kingdom period resembled a Phonician alphabet. The illustration shows a copy of the Siloam Inscription which was placed at the mouth of Hezekiah's Tunnel, August 2010. It is written in Paleo-Hebrew, Phoenician alphabet. The original was found in the tunnel and removed in 1891 to the Istanbul Archaeology Museum, Turkey.

Copy of Paleo-Hebrew Inscription found
in Hezekiah's Tunnel (Phoenician Alphabet)

Ugaritic and Paleo-Hebrew Inscriptions

Before these discoveries this type of bigotry could at least be excused. Now the evidence demands that the Hebrews were at least capable of writing the Old Testament.

Ezekiel and Daniel both had the Word of God during the exile. Though many Jews abandoned the Word of God during the exile in Assyria, Babylon, and Persia, believing Jews spread it throughout these empires.

When the exiles returned to Judah, Ezra read the Word of God to the people. The way the people repented showed that most of them were unfamiliar with the Word of God. Ezra and Nehemiah returned the Word of God to the people. Ezra arranged the documents available to him into the Old Testament we are familiar with.

> The Word of God spoke the universe into existence. ("In the beginning was the Word and the Word was with God and the Word was God. The same was in the beginning with God. All things were made by him; and without him was not any thing made that was made." John 1:1, KJV)

John 1:1 KJV The Word of God spoke the world into existence

Everything we know about the antediluvian world was given to us by Noah, his wife, his sons, and their wives, or by direct revelation from God. This information was handed down through many generations. The book of Job was probably written down before the writings of Moses. Moses had this information plus the traditions of his people, plus the information he learned from Egypt plus what God directly spoke to him. He combined these to write what we know as the Law. Joshua continued record-keeping after the death of Moses. Record-keeping during the period of the Judges was less centralized. When Samuel founded the school of the prophets, these men preserved the works of Moses and Joshua and recorded the works of the Judges. They had the responsibility of sifting through the information they had to be certain that they had the very Word of God. Samuel and the prophets also taught the law to the people and recorded the events of the Kingdom period.

Throughout the kingdom period, good kings proclaimed God's Word and evil kings attacked and destroyed it. The lowest point came during the reigns of Manasseh and his son Amon when every known copy of the Word of God was destroyed. Amon was assassinated and his son Josiah came to the throne. Then a copy of the Word of God was found in the temple. It seems that this was the only copy of God's Word left on earth. Josiah caused the Word of God to be copied and taught throughout Judah and whatever was left of the northern kingdom. Though the thorough destructions by the Assyrians and Babylonians destroyed copies of the Word of God as well as destroying the Hebrew culture, the revivals under Josiah provided many copies of the Word of God throughout the Diaspora.

Men such as Isaiah and Jeremiah were called by God to be writing prophets. Other prophets, such as Elijah and Elisha, performed the office of prophet while leaving the record-keeping to others. Men who did not have the office of prophet were also used to write the Word of God. David, Asaph, and others wrote Psalms. Solomon and others wrote wisdom literature.

After returning from the exile, the priest Ezra collected and edited these documents into the book which we know as the Old Testament. The complete Old Testament was translated into Syriac (Peshitta) as well as Greek (The Septuagint). Both of these are translations and no translation is inspired, though both are helpful in giving insight into the meanings of words and cultures. (see sections on Peshitta and Septuagint)

Fragment of the Syriac Peshitta

The existing Hebrew texts which God has preserved for us today are known as the Masoretic text. Hebrew scribes who counted every character of every copy preserved these texts. Since pronunciation and spelling change through time and the existing Hebrew text has no vowels, these men created a system of vowel points and accents to pass on the Word of God to future generations. Various Jewish groups all over the globe used copies of the Masoretic text for centuries without so much as a change in a single character.

Malachi is the last Old Testament book. Four hundred years passed without any written revelation from God.

The Law, the Prophets, and the Writings

The Divisions of the Hebrew Bible, known by the acronym TaNaKh, or Tanakh, are based on the Masoretic Text. The Masoretic Text was first the Torah, or instruction, the first five books of Moses, the second the Neviim or Prophets, and the third the Ketuvim or Writings.

> *Now he said to them, "These are my words which I spoke to you while I was still with you,*

> *that all things which are written about me in the Law of Moses and the Prophets and the Psalms must be fulfilled."* (Luke 24:4).

Christ appeared to the disciples shortly after His resurrection and He spoke about the Scriptures dealing with Himself. He began with the Torah (The Law of Moses), went next to the Prophets, then on to the Writings, which begins in the Hebrew Bible with Psalms. The books in these categories are as follows:

Torah (Law or Instruction)

Bereishit (In the Beginning) Genesis, Shemot (Names) Exodus, Vayikra (And He Called) Leviticus, Bamidbar (In the Desert) Numbers, Devarim (Words) Deuteronomy

Neviim (Prophets) Joshua, Judges, Samuel (I and II are counted as one book), Kings (I and II are counted as one book), Isaiah, Jeremiah, Ezekiel, Trei Asar (The Twelve) Hosea, Joel, Amos, Obadiah, Jonah, Micah, Nahum, Habakkuk, Zephaniah, Haggai, Zechariah, Malachi

Ketuvim (Writings) Psalms, Proverbs, Job, Song of Songs, Ruth, Lamentations, Ecclesiastes, Esther, Daniel, Ezra (Includes Nehemiah), Chronicles (I and II are counted as one book).

Ugaritic and Ancient Hebrew

Cuneiform is a script made of wedge-shaped impressions in clay tablets. Archaeologists have found tablets written in Sumerian, Akkadian, and Eblaite. Cuneiform is usually a one-sign, one-word script like Chinese. Scholars think it developed from pictogram writing like Egyptian hieroglyphics.

French Archeologists in 1928 found cuneiform tablets at Ras Shamra in Syria near the Mediterranean Sea. Ugarit, an ancient Canaanite city, was built on this site. Ugarit cuneiform used one sign to represent one letter of an alphabet, unlike other cuneiform writings. The Ugarit alphabet was the same as the Hebrew alphabet, as was its language. Hebrew scholars have found studying Ugaritic helpful in understanding some difficult Hebrew Scriptures.

Ugaritic Gods List

Ugarit's tablets are dated by mainstream scholars at about 1300 to 1200 BC. The tablet pictured above lists gods the people worshiped. El, Baal, Asherah, and even Yahweh are named among their gods. Studies of the culture shows it is similar to that of the Hebrews.

because Ugaritic seems to have a common source with Hebrew, its discovery is evidence that Semitic Script, and especially Hebrew writing, is older than scholars originally believed.

(Adapted from "The History of Ugarit," by Jeff A. Benner, from the Ancient Hebrew Research Center website ancient-hebrew.org.)

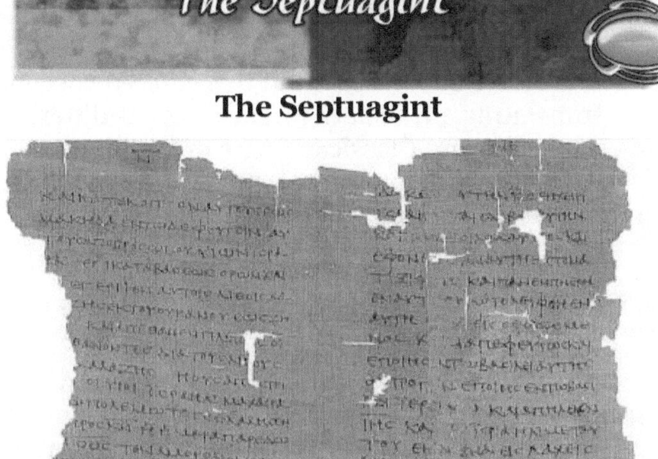

The Septuagint

Dead Sea Scroll of Joshua from the Septuagint

The Septuagint or LXX is a translation of the Hebrew Old Testament into Greek, according to tradition, by seventy scholars (it was named for the Roman numeral 70, LXX) between the 3rd and 2nd centuries in Alexandria, Egypt. Apparently paid for by the Ptolemaic Dynasty along with many other Greek translation works for the library at Alexandria. The Septuagint is quoted from extensively in the New Testament. The writer of Hebrews quoted from it exclusively. In the Septuagint book of

Esther Ahasuerus is Artaxerxes. The apocryphal book Bel and the Dragon is incorporated into Daniel in the LXX and the book of Esther is considerably longer. The Septuagint may have been based on a different Hebrew text than the Masoretic. This idea is supported somewhat by passages in the Dead Sea Scrolls.

Different Codexes of the Septuagint have different books of the Apocrypha included, though almost all have the Maccabees included as Scriptures. Many differences in translations have been found, but this could be because we are translating a translation. The Greek is different from both Koine and Classical. Some of the things we look at as differences may simply be lack of familiarity with the types of Greek used to make the translation.

The order of books in the Septuagint is as follows. Note that some books considered apocryphal today are among those included.

Genesis Exodus Leviticus Numbers Deuteronomy Joshua Judges Ruth Kings I (1st Samuel) Kings II (2nd Samuel) Kings III (1st Kings) Kings IV (2nd Kings) Paralipomenon I (1st Chronicles) Paralipomenon II (2nd Chronicles) Esdras I Esdras II (Ezra) Nehemiah Psalms Prayer of Manasseh Proverbs Ecclesiastes Song of Solomon Job Wisdom of Solomon Wisdom of Sirach (Ecclesiasticus) Esther Judith Tobit Hosea Amos Micah Joel Obadiah Jonah Nahum Habakkuk Zephaniah Haggai Zechariah Malachi Isaiah Jeremiah Baruch Lamentations (of Jeremiah) Epistle of Jeremiah Ezekiel Daniel Song of the Three Children Susanna Bel and the Dragon I Maccabees II Maccabees III Maccabees (Some texts also include IV Maccabees and Psalms of Solomon).

Order of Books in the Septuagint

Genesis
Exodus
Leviticus
Numbers
Deuteronomy
Joshua
Judges
Ruth
Kings I (1st Samuel)
Kings II (2nd Samuel)
Kings III (1st Kings)
Kings IV (2nd Kings)
Paralipomenon I (1st Chronicles)
Paralipomenon II (2nd Chronicles)
Esdras I
Esdras II (Ezra)
Nehemiah
Psalms
Prayer of Manasseh
Proverbs
Ecclesiastes
Song of Solomon
Job
Wisdom of Solomon
Wisdom of Sirach (Ecclesiasticus)
Esther
Judith
Tobit
Hosea
Amos
Micah
Joel
Obadiah
Jonah
Nahum
Habakkuk
Zephaniah
Haggai
Zechariah
Malachi
Isaiah
Jeremiah
Baruch
Lamentations (of Jeremiah)
Epistle of Jeremiah
Ezekiel
Daniel
Song of the Three Children
Susanna
Bel and the Dragon
I Maccabees
II Maccabees
III Maccabees
(Some texts also include IV Maccabees and Psalms of Solomon)

Order of books in Septuagint

The Masoretic Text

The Masoretic Text

The Masoretic text is the authoritative Hebrew Text of the Old Testament, the "official" version of the Hebrew Bible. It established what books are included in the Hebrew Canon and precisely defines the letter-text, plus the proper method of chanting, speaking or singing the text in public readings. The Masorah is the name for this system of preserving the exact text and oral guides. It was copied by Jews known as Masoretes between the 7th and 10th centuries A.D in the cities of Tiberias, Jerusalem, and Babylonia. It has few differences from the accepted texts of the 2nd century and the Qumran (Dead Sea Scrolls) texts but differs in many places from the Septuagint.

Mesorah refers to the passing down of traditions, but in the case of the Masoretic Text it specifically means the diacritic markings in the text and marginal notes intending to preserve an accurate text.

When the Dead Sea Scrolls of Qumran (see section below) were discovered, 60% of the scrolls agreed to a significant degree with the Masoretic texts. One cave, known as Cave Four, contained less-well-preserved scrolls, not kept in jars. In that cave were found most of the variations from the Masoretic text, such as Septuagint-supporting texts, but also some fragments which conformed most closely to it.

Masoretic Text Aleppo Codex

The Syriac Peshitta

The Syriac Peshitta

The Syriac Peshitta is a translation of the Bible into Syriac, or Aramaic. Origen, an early biblical scholar, made a translation/commentary work including the Hebrew Old Testament and his revision of the Septuagint around 200 AD, called the Hexapla. Later, a Syriac translation of the Old Testament called the Syrohexapla was done from Origen's Septuagint. The Peshitta (which means simple or clear) came into use in the late 800's AD but no one knows for certain where or when the translation work was done. The Old Testament was done separately and much earlier than the New Testament, probably by Jews, but scholars are uncertain when or where for either Old or New Testaments. It may be that some New Testament quotes of Old Testament verses are from the Peshitta. The Old Testament Syriac contains the same books as the Hebrew but in a different order.

Fragment of Syriac Peshitta

This translation is, like all translations, not inspired, but it is very helpful in studying the Scriptures for understanding culture, for textual comparison purposes, and for aids to meaning. It is a very old and accurate translation.

The Dead Sea Scrolls

Between 1947 and 1956, almost 900 scrolls written on parchment or papyrus were discovered in 11 caves near Qumran on the West Bank of the Jordan River. Theories about who lived there vary based on archaeological studies. Some areas of habitation at the site are simple and Spartan but there are also evidences of wealth and worldly relationships. Some archaeologists think it was a fort, part of a series of forts throughout the area. Theories about the Essenes, a Jewish sect of ascetics written about by Josephus, Pliny the Elder, and Philo, have been questioned. The scrolls themselves mention a group called the Yahad about which nothing is really known. Some say a wealthy villa-owner gave sanctuary to those fleeing Jerusalem and offered hiding places for the scrolls formerly kept there. Clearly they made pottery and stored and copied scrolls. Phylacteries, Mezuzahs, (items containing portions of the Scriptures worn on the body or placed on the door of a house by Jews) inscribed pottery, and unidentifiable document fragments have also been found in the caves. Little else is known for certain about who lived or worked there.

Isaiah Scroll Qumran

Many of the scrolls are very detailed, with strict rules and regulations for conducting worship and living in a Jewish community. These differed from the way most Jews were living at the time. Some are commentaries on biblical books. Some are hymns and additions to the biblical feasts and ceremonies. Some may deal with eschatology (the end times, like Revelation), and others are considered apocryphal today.

One item is a copper scroll, very different from all the others, which seems to be a kind of treasure map, mentioning large amounts of gold, silver, and coins, but it cannot be shown to have any biblical importance. Some have speculated that it may be the treasures from the Temple at Jerusalem and even include the Ark of the Covenant. Most of the directions are very detailed but concern structures or places that cannot be identified and seem no longer to exist.

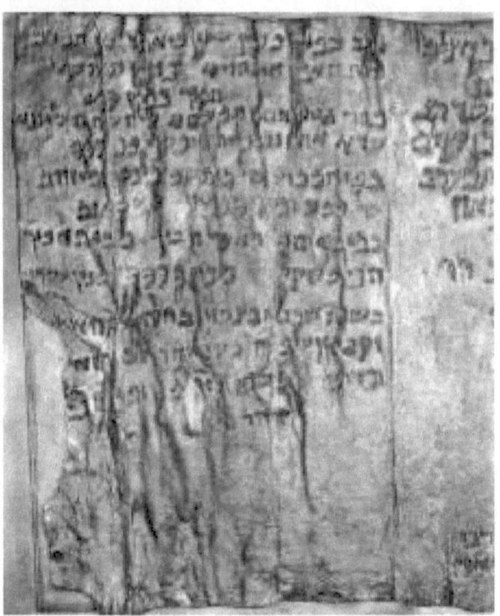

Copper Scroll Qumran

The important point is that other scrolls include some of the oldest known manuscripts of the Holy Scriptures. Here is a list of partial or complete Scripture texts found in the caves. Many of these are just fragments, especially the ones found in Cave Four. See other appendixes for their importance. The Book of Isaiah is the only one that exists as one complete copy.

Some copies of books are called "Paleo" versions because they are written in a different, supposedly earlier form of Hebrew script. Some copies are Septuagint versions.

All the Old Testament books, with the possible exception of Esther, are represented in some portion among the Dead Sea Scrolls. Below is an example of how many copies or partial copies of some of the books are among the collection.

Psalms--39 Deuteronomy--33 Genesis--24 Isaiah--22 Exodus--18 Leviticus--17 Numbers--11 Minor

Prophets--10 Daniel--8 Jeremiah--6 Ezekiel--6 Job--6 1&2—Samuel -- 4

Manuscripts related to (or claimed to be related to) the Scriptures

Manuscripts claiming relationship to the Scriptures

(Author's note. There are so many false and heretical manuscripts presented as "significant" in the study of the Scriptures to list and describe here. This is only a list of some of the ones that actually have a claim to authority or have people who persist in pushing them as authoritative but are false.

Jerome's Latin Vulgate

In 382, Pope Damascus commissioned Jerome to translate the Bible into Latin, which had become the language of European scholarship. For the Versio Vulgata (common translation) Jerome worked from Hebrew and from the Septuagint for the Old Testament. His work took twenty years. He did not complete the New Testament. That work was done later by others and incorporated into his work. It became the standard translation for the Western church after Jerome's death but was not popular during his lifetime.

Augustine protested the Hebrew basis for the translation. He said it would divide the Eastern and Western churches because the Septuagint was preferred in the East. He pointed to an incident where a bishop in Tripoli preached on Jonah from the Vulgate and people rioted in the streets. The Vulgate was the first book printed in moveable type on Gutenberg's printing press. The translation into Latin may have been commissioned or later used with the idea of preventing people from reading and understanding the Bible for themselves, forcing them to go to a priest for interpretation. It has flaws, and it is not inspired. However, the Latin Vulgate may be the translation through which more people have come to Christ than any other.

Medieval Illustration of Jerome

The Cairo Genizah

The Cairo Genizah was a storage building of the Ben Ezra Synagogue in Fustat (Old Cairo) Egypt. Hundreds of thousands of manuscripts were stored there because of the custom of Jews not to discard any documents related to the Scriptures or their study without a special burial ceremony. 25,000 Hebrew Bible fragments were stored there along with many records in many languages, religious, historical, and simple business transactions. Many have yet to be catalogued or studied.

Cairo Geniza Interior and Exterior Photos

The Nash Papyrus

Nash Papyrus Fragment

This papyrus was found in Egypt in 1898. It is believed to date to about 150-100 B.C., making it the oldest known Hebrew manuscript before the Dead Sea Scrolls were found. It consists of four sheets containing the Ten Commandments with portions drawn from Exodus 20 and Deuteronomy 5, followed by Deuteronomy 6:4's "Hear O Israel, the Lord Our God is One," called by Jews the "Shema." It follows the Septuagint in this method of presentation. The Talmud records this manuscript as representing the worship practice of Egyptian Jews at that time. It is important because it gives support to the Septuagint translation in one respect where it differs from the Masoretic text. It currently resides in the Cambridge Library.

The Nag Hammadi Library are texts discovered near the Upper Egyptian town of Nag Hammadi. In 1945 twelve leather bound papyrus codices were found buried in a sealed jar. This collection included Coptic works translated from Greek. Some are pagan, one combining the worship of Hermes and Thoth. One is part of Plato's *Republic.* It also has an apocryphal work called the "Gospel of Thomas." The collection is kept at the Coptic Museum in Cairo. The Gospel of Thomas exists in partial copies in other places and is used by liberals to discredit the authority of the true Canon of Scriptures as proof of the existence of the "Q" document. These texts are believed to have been buried in response to the preaching of Eusebius and Athanasius against unscriptural texts.

Nag Hammadi Library and Gospel of Thomas Page

Church Fathers' Writings

These include The Letter of Clement I, the Didachae (The Lord's Teaching to the Twelve Apostles Through the Nations) and The First Apology of Justin Martyr. These were on some lists to be included in the New Testament Scriptures, but are now considered part of a group of writings called "Early Church Fathers." These are Christian writings of people who lived or wrote just after the time Christ was alive on earth, but are not considered eyewitness or first-person recordings of His earthly life and teachings. Some knew the Apostles or other followers of Christ personally. Their works are good teaching but not Scriptures.

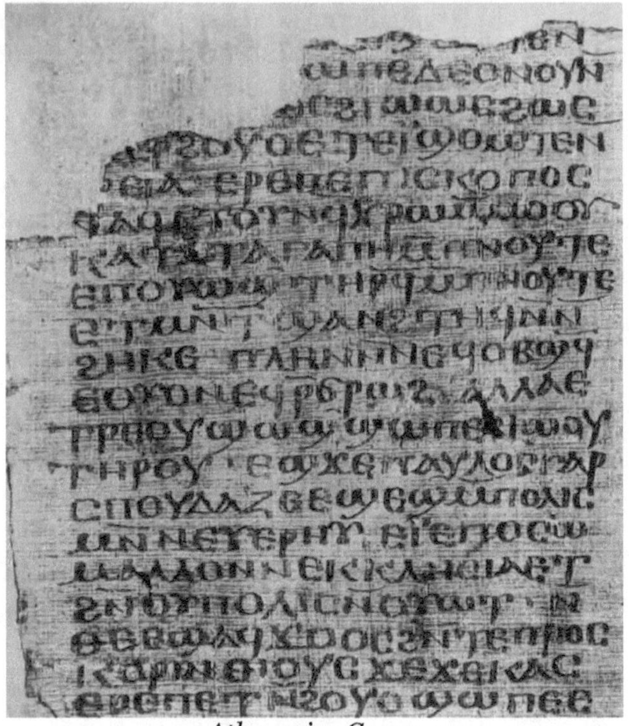

Athenasius Canon

There are many works that are considered religious, related in some way to Judaism or Christianity, or sects or cults of these religions, and it is impossible to list or explain them all. Jewish literature includes such works as the Talmud, the Midrash, the Kaballah, and others. Sometimes these are commentaries, sometimes historical or scribal records. They sometimes record customs and traditions which became revered. Sometimes hey are mystical works promoting false belief. The Apocrypha usually refers to specific books related to the Old or New Testaments. Some of these have factual history, some are fiction, some were prayerfully excluded from the canon after much consideration by godly men. Other works have been proved to be forgeries. (This last includes some of the works that go by the name of “the Book of Jasher”. Please see our Conflict of the Ages series for more information about extrabiblical works.). Many works promote erroneous views or heresies. Some are used to undermine the authority of true Scriptures.

Elephantine Papyri

Elephantine Ruins and Papyrus Sample

These were manuscripts found on the island of Elephantine in the Nile River. A community of Jews lived there around the time others were returning to Israel to rebuild the temple in Ezra and Nehemiah's time. These Jews did not seek to return to the land and seemed to have had many corrupt worship practices, even to building their own temple on the island. Although none of the manuscripts found there actually contain parts of the Scriptures, there are letters addressed to Persian rulers and even to Sanballat the Horonite (mentioned in the Scriptures as persecuting the returning Jews). These confirm that the Aramaic of Ezra was being used at least as early as the fifth century BC. Liberal scholars have tried to put Ezra as late as the third century.

Old Testament Part One Review Questions

(Note that for the multiple choice there may be more than one correct answer.)

Multiple Choice

Multiple Choice

B 1. An ancient language in which the Bible has been written is

A. Hittite B. Syriac C. Ugaritic D. Egyptian

A 2. was the king given the last copy of God's Word at that time.

A. Josiah B. Ammon C. Hezekiah D. Manasseh

C 3. collected the books into the Old Testament .

A. Elijah B. Ezekiel C. Ezra D. Elimelech

A 4. The Diaspora was

A. Jews scattered into other countries B. A translation of the Scriptures C. A heretical teaching D. A priestly garment

Matching
(Some answers are in the Bible History Section)

Matching

A. Vulgate B. Septuagint C. Tunnel Inscription D. Egyptian E. Jewish F. Oldest Writing G. like Hebrew H. Peshitta

C 1. Phonecian Script

G 2. Ugaritic

H 3. Syriac

B 4. Greek

F 5. Cuneiform

D 6. Coptic

E 7. Hebrew

A 8. Latin

Short Answer

1. What are the three divisions of the Hebrew Bible mentioned by Jesus Christ? *Law of Moses, Prophets, Psalms/Writings*

2. Arrange the books of the Old Testament into the three divisions, using a Bible's Table of Contents if needed. *See the section on **The Law, the Prophets, and the Writings** for the correct order.*

3. What makes the Cuneiform tablets found at Ras Shamra good Bible study aids? *They are in Ugaritic, a language very much like Hebrew.*

4. Where was the Septuagint supposedly translated, and by how many people? *Alexandria, seventy*

5. Which book in the New Testament quotes only from the Septuagint version of the Old Testament? *Hebrews*

True or False

T 1. The Ptolemaic Dynasty commissioned the Septuagint translation.

F 2. Many Old Testament books have apocryphal books added to them in the Septuagint.

T 3. The Dead Sea Scrolls help support the Septuagint's translations.

T 4. The Masoretic text includes markings to aid proper pronunication in oral reading.

F 5. Mesorah means only traditional customs.

Matching

From the Septuagint section: Apocrypha or Scriptural Canon?

Put an A next to Apocryphal books and a C next to Scriptural Canon Books *(Warning! Some titles are not from the English version.)*

C 1. Paralipomenon I

A 2. Esdras II

A 3. Wisdom of Solomon

C 4. Daniel

A 5. Ecclesiasticus

A 6. Tobit

C 7. Haggai

C 8. Joel

A 9. Wisdom of Solomon

A 10. Judith

Multiple Choice

C 1. The Jews who copied the authoritative Hebrew Old Testament texts were known as

A. Tiberians B. Qumrans C. Masoretes D. Mesorahs

B 2. What percentage of the dead Sea Scrolls agree with the authoritative Hebrew Old Testament texts?

A. 30% B. 60% C. 90% D. 100%

A 3. The word Peshitta means

A. simple or clear B. having six parts C. made by Origen D. written in Syria

D 4. As a translation, the Syrica Peshitta is

A. Relatively recent B. Not inspired C. very old, very accurate D. B and C

B 5. Qumran is

A. on the East Bank of the Jordan River B. Where the Dead Sea Scrolls were found C. a system of fifty caves D. All of the above

B 6. Who did not mention the Essenes?

A. Josephus B. Pliny the Younger C. Pliny the Elder D. Philo

A,D 7. We know for certain that the caves at Qumran were occupied by (more than one correct answer is possible)

A. Copyists B. Essenes C. Yahad D. Potters

D 8. The Copper Scroll is

A. different from all others B. uncertain biblical importance C. possibly a treasure map D. all of the above

C 9. Why is it important to find the oldest manuscripts of the Scriptures?

A. To keep archaeologists busy B. To better refute heresies C. To ensure our Bible is as accurate as possible D. To improve study of ancient languages.

B 10. The word Vulgate means

A. from Damascus B. Common C. Latin D. Translation

D 11. Genizah is

A. A city in Egypt B. A type of papyrus C. A Hebrew house D. A storage building

A 12. The oldest bible manuscript before the finding of the Dead Sea Scrolls was

A. the Nash Papyrus B. the Nag Hammadi Library C. The Elephantine Payrus D. the Septuagint

D 13. The Nag Hammadi Library is written in

A. Hebrew B. Greek . C. Athenasian D. Coptic

D 14. The Gospel of Thomas is

A. Part of the New Testament B. Part of the Apocrypha C. possibly a forgery using the Apostle Thomas' name D. B and C

D 15. Which of the following are part of the Hebrew Old Testament Scriptures?

A. Talmud B. Midrash C. Kaballah D. Ketuvim

A 16. What makes the Elephantine Papyri important?

A. Documents contemporary with Ezra B. Written in Egyptian Hieroglyphics C. showing Jewish idolatry D. Confirms the Diaspora

Research/Thought/Essay Questions

Research/Thought/Essay Questions

These are extra credit, enrichment, thought, and essay questions. The teacher can decide which ones to use, if any, and how long essays should be. Answers will vary, but grading should be based on good writing mechanics, real information, research, and clearly described sources. We suggest handwritten essays for these shorter assignments, not computer-generated.

1. Write an essay about either Isaac Newton or William of Occam and their ideas expressed in the quotations at the beginning of this study. Include three sources.

Newton's quote comes from an Untitled Treatise on Revelation, available online at

https://www.newtonproject.ox.ac.uk/view/texts/normalized/THEM00137

under the section Rules for Methodizing/Construing the Apocalypse, point 9. Newton had many religious writings that were never published while he lived. It is a fairly long work with old language and spelling but the student should be able to get some ideas from the treatise or from many other works written about Newton and his religious writings.

William of Occam actually said "Plurality must never be posited without necessity," in the theological commentary on the Sentences of Peter Lombard. The statement has been paraphrased many different ways. The work itself does not seem to be available for free online, but many articles have been written about Occam, or Ockham, including quotes from it, and a student should not have difficulty finding source material.

The teacher might even want to encourage students to explore the fact that both these men wrote in a context of religious study, yet the words are usually applied to Science, and comment on why this might be so.

2. Find two people (writers, scientists, theologians) who have rejected the 2 Timothy 3:16 verse and explain how they justify doing so.

Charles Harold Dodd (7 April 1884 3. – 21 September 1973), who directed the translation of the New English Bible, is one possible subject. Rudolf Karl Bultmann (August 20, 1884 – July 30, 1976), who said History and Faith have no relationship to each other, is another person who rejected inspiration.

Find sources for two arguments against the Bible having a true historical chronology, state their positions, and find evidence to refute them from conservative scholars.

http://www.answersingenesis.org/articles/am/v6/n1/chronology-wars is a good article about a biblical perspective on Chronology using ancient sources. http://www.newadvent.org/cathen/03731a.htm Is a Roman Catholic website which insists the world is millions of years old and gives several "scholars" who back up that view, along with a chronology of the Bible which will be a useful jumping-off point for research on this topic.

History of chronologies site

https://nabataea.net/explore/biblicalstudies/biblicalhistory/early-chronologies-of-the-bible/

4. Write a short paper (1-2 pages) on the oral tradition in literature. Briefly record one or two accounts you find that are similar to the Thoth/Ammon/writing account from Plato. Research a modern (last 200 years) example of the use of oral transmission using one of the examples in this work (gang members, prisoners of war, inmates, or spies). How can the oral method of learning be useful or even necessary to preserve important knowledge?

Lycurgus, ruler of ancient Sparta, did not allow his laws to be written down, so his is an example of the oral tradition. Plutarch's Life of Lycurgus, translated by John Dryden and others, 1683 is available free on many sites like Gutenberg.org. Two other possible peoples to research on oral tradition are Maori literature and India's voluminous ancient writings.

http://www.sacred-texts.com The Internet Sacred Text Archive is a rich resource for ancient writings, especially of a religious nature. They sell the latest version of everything on the site for 99.95, over 1700 texts with illustrations. Frankly, J.B. Hare, the site founder, died fairly recently and the future of the site is uncertain. Everything on line is available for free, but the price of the disk is still worth it if these resources cease to be available from this site.

5. What is the Diaspora? Find evidence that these people had the Word of God to communicate to others.

The Diaspora is the Jewish people dispersed by wars, the destructions of Samaria and Judah, and the Fall of Jerusalem. Some were taken captive by conquerors, some escaped advancing armies into other countries. The education of young Jewish boys (and sometimes girls) included memorizing most of the Torah (the first five books of the Bible) and older students learned even more of the Scriptures. These memorized scriptures they could always take with them and communicate to others. Phylacteries and Mezzuzahs were objects Jews either wore or placed by the doors of their houses. These contained written Scriptures, though only small portions. Caches of manuscripts (see our appendixes in this file) show that thousands of copies of portions of the Scriptures existed in the Middle East.

6. Find at least three examples in the Pentateuch (Genesis-Deuteronomy) that records may have been written down or passed on orally before the Law was given at Mt. Sinai or that people were taught something about what God expected of them before Moses.

Exodus 13: 9 says that the Passover feast will be a memorial "a sign unto thee upon thine hand, and for a memorial between thine eyes, that the Lord's law may be in thy mouth." This is similar to other passages from which the custom of phylacteries came, writing down the Word and wearing it on the hands and forehead. It implies that they were already writing down God's laws.

Exodus 17:14 is the first time God directly tells someone (Moses) to write something down. This is the promise to utterly destroy Amalek and comes before the arrival at Sinai. God says Moses is to write it in a book, and rehearse it in the ears (repeat it orally) of Joshua. This assumes they already understood writing and were familiar with keeping important records of events.

Other possibilities are Genesis Ch 4, when God did not accept Cain's offering. There must have been some understanding of God's expectations, passed on by Adam to his sons, or this incident wouldn't have occurred. Abel knew what sacrifice was acceptable. God would not have said what He did to Cain if he didn't know better.

http://www.answersingenesis.org/articles/2007/01/25/genesis-evolution-not-mixIn Point 17 of this article says, "Adam Could Write." Genesis 5:1, it says "These are the generations of Adam." Many scholars believe that Adam himself wrote this. They say his and other writings were preserved by Noah on the ark, and that Moses may actually have had access to copies of writings of the people who lived before him since creation. The clay tablets found at the ancient city of Ugarit (see the appendix on Ugarit and Ancient Hebrew) show a language identical to Hebrew written in cuneiform. Cuneiform is believed to be the first kind of writing and was used by many ancient cultures. It may be that Adam wrote Hebrew in cuneiform.

7. Lycurgus is supposed to have turned Sparta into a perfect society. Research to find out at least three ways in which his practices were contrary to Scriptural principles.

The account of Lycurgus is recorded in Plutarch, from his Life of Lycurgus, translated by John Dryden and others, 1683. Many sites such as Gutenberg have this work online in text form. 1. He encouraged girls to dance naked in festival parades in front of boys. 2. He also segregated the boys into training camps where they were supposed to steal food and were punished only if they were caught. 3. They were also encouraged to have sex, with girls or boys, without any thought of marriage. 4. Married couples could share the wife with another man if the husband was too old or unable to produce children. There are other many examples.

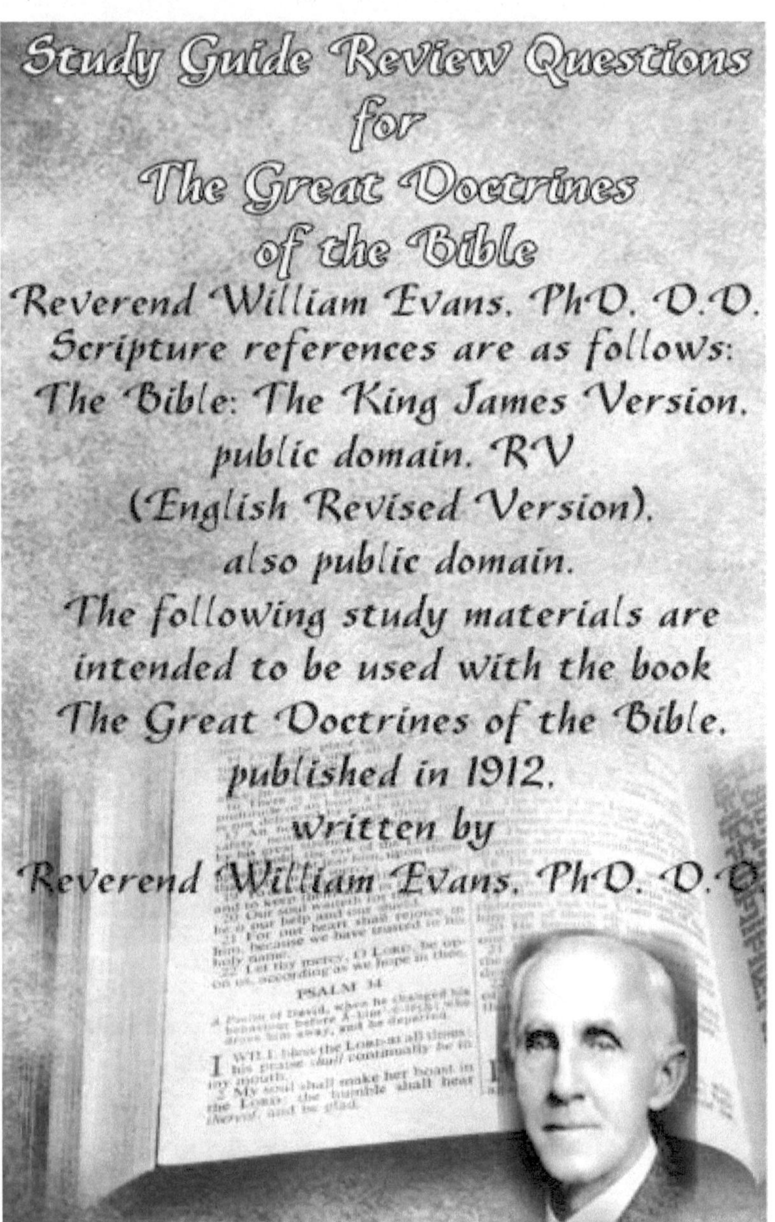

Reverend William Evans, PhD, D.D.

Study Guide Review Questions for The Great Doctrines of the Bible

Scripture references are as follows: The Bible: The King James Version, public domain. RV (English Revised Version), also public domain.

The following study materials are intended to be used with the book *The Great Doctrines of the Bible*, published in 1912, written by Reverend William Evans, PhD, D.D.

1. How to obtain a free electronic copy of Evans for use with this study guide.

The book is available free on Gutenberg.org. The Mobipocket reader is free to download online and will work as a reader interface on most computers if you prefer mobi format. The ePub version works on most other readers. Text, .pdf, and HTML versions will work on any computer.

2. How to use any Evans version with this study

Since we have written our materials with economy in mind and encourage teachers and students to obtain free or as inexpensive materials as possible, we will not refer to page numbers in the works being studied. Page numbers will vary according to the edition the student and teacher use, and in ebooks are variable depending on screen size, text size, and other factors. For Evans we have copied his outline into the study guide by sections. The teacher and student should be able to find the place referred to.

3. Kinds of questions and how to use/grade them.

Generally the questions are in a True/False, Matching, Multiple Choice or Short Answer/Fill-in-the-Blank format. The sections vary greatly in length, from 5 questions to 25 or more. Not all answers can be found directly in the text. In some cases the student will have to look up Scripture passages noted and find the answer in the content of the verse. More extensive essay, research and thought questions are included in the teacher's guide and can be assigned as the teacher chooses. There are no lesson plans. The teacher decides the pace at which to cover the material. He/she may select questions to use as daily assignments, quizzes, tests, review exercises, or projects as desired, or simply have the student work through the book and questions from beginning to end. The teacher can assign ten questions at one point each, one essay at fifty or one hundred points, or any combination of points per question that makes a percentage grade easy to obtain.

4. Note to the teacher on grading the assignments.

Answer keys are provided in the teacher's guide but there are no explanations for why an answer is "True" or "False" or why a choice is correct or another choice is wrong. Usually this is clear from Evans' text or the Scriptures. The teacher can use good judgment if something seems unclear. The essay/research/thought questions include suggestions for areas to research and in some cases partial answers but these are for the teacher to decide on as far as what constitutes a "complete" assignment. Length and scope can be limited based on the student's ability or desire or the teacher's ability or available time to check correctness and completeness.

5. Authors' Note concerning Evans' language, style and content.

Most of Evans' text uses the KJV. We use KJV in any Scriptures included by us. Evans does, however, refer to and sometimes quote from the English Revised Version Bible.

http://www.twmodules.com/bibles/bibles-word-for-word/english-revised-version/ includes a good description of the RV Bible. Note that Evans states in the text that "The Revised Version translation of 2 Timothy 3:16 is erroneous," and makes his point with considerable detail and emphasis. He has not replaced the KJV with the RV but simply uses what he believes to be the most accurate rendering of a verse on the occasions when he uses the RV in preference to the KJV.

The "Great Doctrines" book was written in 1912, based on Evans' teaching career, and the language and style is somewhat difficult reading. Evans also brings a good deal of philosophy into his work and the reader is sometimes left scratching his/her head about the meaning of some of his statements and people he chooses to quote. A good example of this is from The Doctrine of God, I. The Existence of God, 1. Assumed by the Scriptures. "A God capable of proof would be no God at all" (Jacobi). This is really gibberish. Fortunately Evans follows this with clear, solid Scriptures. "He is the self-existent One (Exodus 3:14) and the Source of all life (John 5:26). The sublime opening of the Scriptures announces the fact of God and His existence: 'In the beginning God' (Genesis 1:1)."

Evans is one of the simplest and easiest to read among Doctrines writers. Compare him to Hodges or Thiessen and you will come to appreciate his relative simplicity. He breaks down the Doctrines into outline form and supports them throughout with Scriptures, as he says in the quote below.

"It is intended that the doctrines of this book should be studied side by side with the open Bible. ... There must be constant reference to the Scriptures themselves."

Evans says this in the foreword to his book. He also says, "The demand for this book has come from the students in the classroom who have listened to these lectures on the Great Doctrines of the Bible, and have desired and requested that they be put into permanent form for the purpose of further study and reference. This volume is prepared, therefore, primarily, but not exclusively, for the student, and with his needs in mind."

When Evans speaks of students, keep in mind that he taught at Moody Bible Institute primarily, so he is speaking of post-high-school level students. His work is still one of the easiest of doctrines books to understand.

Evans also lists related works that he consulted in the writing of his book. What the Bible Teaches, by R. A. Torrey, D. D. Systematic Theology, by A. H. Strong, D. D. Christian Doctrine, by Dr. F. L. Patton. The Problem of the Old Testament, and The Christian View of God and the World, by Dr. James Orr; Studies in Christian Doctrine, by George Knapp; Jesus and the Gospel, and The Death of Christ, by Prof. James Denny; The Person and Work of Jesus, by Nathan E. Wood, D. D.

6. In Case of Disagreement

It should be noted that good men disagree on certain details of presentation in any study of the Bible. The teacher and/or student may disagree with Evans, or with the authors of this study, on some points. In a few cases, we have written commentary or explanations where we believe Evans is hard to understand, unclear, or incorrect in the way he presents some of his material. These are not major disagreements. These are simply places where good people can be confused or actually differ. Most of these instances do not make any difference to the study and are simply informational.

Following is a list of the various outline sections of Evans' work included in this text.

THE DOCTRINE OF GOD

THE DOCTRINE OF JESUS CHRIST

THE DOCTRINE OF THE HOLY SPIRIT

THE DOCTRINE OF MAN

THE DOCTRINES OF SALVATION

Repentance--Faith--Regeneration--Justification--Adoption--Sanctification--Prayer

THE DOCTRINE OF THE CHURCH

THE DOCTRINE OF THE SCRIPTURES

THE DOCTRINE OF ANGELS

THE DOCTRINE OF SATAN

THE DOCTRINE OF THE LAST THINGS

The Second Coming of Christ--The Resurrection--The Judgment--The Destiny of the Wicked--The Reward of the Righteous

The Doctrine of God

THE DOCTRINE OF GOD

I. THE EXISTENCE OF GOD: (vs. Atheism).

1. ASSUMED BY THE SCRIPTURES.

2. PROOFS OF THE EXISTENCE OF GOD.

a) Universal belief in the Existence of God.

b) Cosmological:--Argument from Cause.

c) Teleological:--Argument from Design.

d) Ontological:--Argument from Being.

e) Anthropological:--Moral Argument.

f) Argument from Congruity.

g) Argument from Scripture.

II. THE NATURE OF GOD: (Vs. Agnosticism)

1. THE SPIRITUALITY OF GOD: (Vs. Materialism).

2. THE PERSONALITY OF GOD: (Vs. Pantheism).

3. THE UNITY OF GOD: (vs. Polytheism).

4. THE TRINITY: (vs. Unitarianism).

III. THE ATTRIBUTES OF GOD.

1. THE NATURAL ATTRIBUTES:

a) Omniscience.

b) Omnipotence.

c) Omnipresence.

d) Eternity.

2. THE MORAL ATTRIBUTES:

a) Holiness.

b) Righteousness.

c) Faithfulness.

d) Mercy and Loving-kindness.

e) Love.

Depiction of God by Michelangelo

The writers of Scriptures did not attempt to prove the existence of God. “Everywhere and at all times it is a fact taken for granted.” This is not strictly true, but as the study progresses the student should pick up on places where the Scriptures state proofs of God’s existence and reality. Evans also says that the Scriptures do not allow for atheists. “Psalm 14:1: ‘The fool hath said in his heart. There is no God,’ indicates not a disbelief in the existence, but rather in the active interest of God in the affairs of men.’ Many other passages indicate that man thinks God is not paying attention to what he does and Evans says this is the true mindset of the so-called atheist or agnostic. Man has convinced himself that God does not operate the way man thinks he should, and so dismisses Him.

Matching

Match the verse with the aspect of God

A. Seems to hide from man's affairs B. Disbelief in God's interest in man C. Men have more than casual knowledge of God D. The self-existent One E. Source of all life F. The fact of God's existence

D 1. Exodus 3:14

E 2. John 5:26

B 3. Psalm 14:1

A 4. Job 22:12-14

C 5. Romans 1:18-19

F 6. Genesis 1:1

It is true that we can only present evidence. We cannot convince one who rejects the evidence. So it is with acknowledgement of God. "So we say of the existence of God. These arguments are probable, not demonstrative." He says his evidences are cumulative and must be taken step by step, like a building project. When he uses the phrase "our primitive conviction of God's existence," it is best to take this as meaning what is basic or foundational, what is taught to a child early in life, one of the building blocks upon which later knowledge is built. Evans goes into an extended philosophical discussion with quotes which is difficult to understand and does not have much application to the present doctrinal study.

Enkidu and Gilgamesh

His arguments that everyone actually believes in God are also not relevant. It should be noted that making a crude representation of God is not encouraging as an evidence of some kind of "innate" true belief. Man has been making idols to replace God for centuries and has not been groping to crudely understand the true God in very many cases. The analogies about disabilities and knowledge of arithmetic are more useful. Just because some people, "primitive" or "civilized," do not believe in God does not mean He does not exist. Evans brings up many examples of skeptics or atheists contradicting their disbelief but again they are not relevant to this study.

True or False

T 1. Scripture writers do not seek to prove that God exists.

F 2. According to Evans, Scriptures teach that there are men who do not believe in God.

T 3. Evans says that part of belief in God is man's knowledge of his moral responsibility toward God.

T 4. Evans says man knows within himself that God requires propitiation (something by which man may be made acceptable to God).

F 5. Evans believes we have to prove the existence of God to unbelievers.

F 6. Evans says the fossil record goes back 60,000 years.

The arguments in this section state that belief in God is part of the makeup of human beings. While there is evidence of this, even in certain biological studies, and it makes sense from a standpoint of God creating man for fellowship and communion, this section is, again, difficult to understand and not relevant to the study. He does make some good arguments against uniformitarianism, evolution and the eternality of the universe.

Multiple Choice

Multiple Choice

Select from the following possible answers matching the quotes from Evans' "Arguments for the Existence of God." Write the letter of the correct choice beside the number of each question. (answers could be used more than once).

A. Universality of Belief in the Existence of God B. The Argument from Cause (Cosmological) C. Argument from Design (Teleological) D. Argument from Being (Ontological) E. Moral Argument (Anthropological) F. Argument from Congruity G. Argument from Scripture

C 1. "A watch proves not only a maker, an artificer, but also a designer; a watch is made for a purpose."

B 2. No matter how long a vertical chain you have, there must be a staple (fastening) from which it depends (hangs).

D 3. Man has an idea of an infinite and perfect Being.

A 4. All the evidence points to the conclusive fact that this universal faith in the existence of God is innate in man, and comes from rational intuition.

F 5. If we have a theory which fits all the facts in the case, we know then that we have the right theory.

G 6. A man cannot deny the truth of the testimony of the Bible unless he says plainly: "No amount of testimony will convince me of the supernatural."

E 7. Man has an emotional nature; only a Being of goodness, power, love, wisdom and holiness could satisfy such a nature, and these things denote the existence of a personal God.

G 8. The preacher may, therefore, safely follow the example of the Scripture in assuming that there is a God.

B 9. The doctrine of the eternity of man cannot be supported. Fossil remains extend back but 6,000 years.

E 10. They imply the existence of a Moral Governor to whom we are responsible. Conscience,—there it is in the breast of man, an ideal Moses thundering from an invisible Sinai the Law of a holy Judge.

True or False

*T*1. To worship God in spirit means worship does not have physical limitations.

F 2. To worship God in truth means to do your best with the knowledge you have.

*F*3. When Jesus appeared to his Disciples after the resurrection, He was a spirit.

*T*4. "God is spirit" means in part that God has no physical limitations.

*F*5. Moses said in Deuteronomy 4:15 that God showed his form to the people in the fire at Horeb.

*T*6. Evans interprets Isaiah 40:25 to mean that making an idol reduces God to something material.

*T*7. "LaPlace swept the heavens with his telescope, but could not find anywhere a God. He might just as well have swept a kitchen with his broom." This means that we cannot "see" God no matter how we look for Him.

*F*8. Man "made in the image of God" can only have one possible meaning according to Evans.

*T*9. God is described as having arms, eyes, ears so that limited humans can understand Him better.

*F*10. The Angel of the Lord is an angel God chose to represent Him on earth.

*F*11. Evans states that there are a few exceptions to John 1:18; "No man hath seen God at any time."

lighted hands

Evans' discussion of the personality of God is another difficult philosophical treatise, but it is important to define the God of the Scriptures to exclude heresies that want an impersonal, uninvolved god as well as those that try to give man some status as part of God. Both give man an excuse to avoid responsibility and accountability toward God and rob God of most of His true nature. He is real, personal, involved, and also embodies the perfections of all the great and admirable qualities man seeks in a father, friend and ruler. These are clearly presented in the Scriptures in this section.

Matching

(In column one are the names of God, repeated twice. In the first set for column two are the meanings of the names. In the second set for column two are the Scriptures which use these names. In the spaces beside the names, place the capital letter of the meaning in 1-7 and in 8-14 place the lower-case letter of the verse.)

A. The Lord our Banner B. The Lord that healeth C. The Lord my Shepherd D. The Lord is present E. The Lord will provide F. The Lord our Righteousness G. The Lord our Peace

E 1. Jehovah-Jireh

B 2. Jehovah-Rapha

A 3. Jehovah-Nissi

G 4. Jehovah-Shalom

C 5.Jehovah-Ra-ah

F 6. Jehovah-Tsidkenu

D 7. Jehovah-Shammah

In 8-14 place the lower-case letter of the verse.

a. Ezekiel 48:35 b. Exodus 15:26 c. Exodus 17:8-15 d. Genesis 22:13, 14 e. Jeremiah 23:6 f. Psalm 23:1 g. Judges 6:24

d 8. Jehovah-Jireh

b 9. Jehovah-Rapha

c 10. Jehovah-Nissi

g 11. Jehovah-Shalom

f 12. Jehovah-Ra-ah

e 13. Jehovah-Tsidkenu

a 14. Jehovah-Shammah

Evans' statements on the personal attributes continue with some good, biblically-supported comparisons and contrasts with idols. He refutes Deism, and shows the level of detail to which God's care for His creation extends.

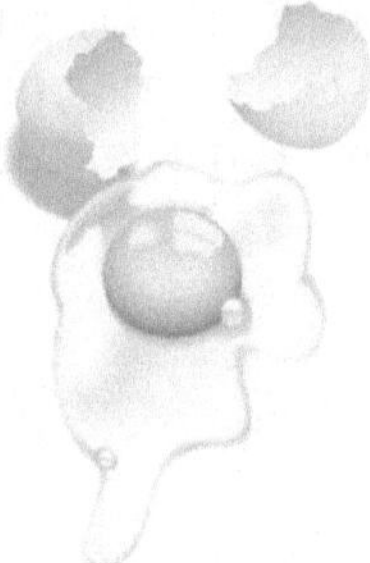

broken egg

Evans' study of the Trinity excludes the possibility of polytheism, tri-theism and dualism. It also explains that the underlying Hebrew words used for God allow for plurality. His proposal that the Trinity can be explained by concepts like two becoming one in marriage and a cluster of grapes, among others, are not really good examples, however. An illustration often used of the Trinity is that of an egg, having a shell, white, and yolk all in the same substance, all equal in importance and co-existent, but this is still a fairly poor example. The verses he uses in support of the Trinity itself are excellent.

grapes

Evans makes a statement under Omnipresence that may cause confusion. He says, "This does not mean that God is everywhere present in the same sense. ... We may summarize the doctrine of the Trinity thus: God the Father is specially manifested in heaven; God the Son has been specially manifested on the earth; God the Spirit is manifested everywhere." This statement does not seem to mean Evans is limiting God's omnipresence, just attempting to explain how the different parts of the Trinity operate as shown in the Scriptures.

Please note that the material for c) Faithfulness appears to be missing from the digital versions of the book available free online. Although it may be intact in the print versions of Evans, it is not included in this study guide to prevent confusion and difficulty for those who do not have access to it.

Fill in the Blank

before each of the following verses dealing with Attributes of God with either N for Natural Attribute or M for Moral Attribute. (Choices will be used more than once)

*M*1. Proverbs 15:9

*N*2. Genesis 18:14

*N*3. Psalm 147:5

*N*4. Habakkuk 1:12

*M*5. Matthew 3:17

*N*6. Psalm 99:9

*N*7. Job 42:2

*M*8. Deuteronomy 4:31

*N*9. Proverbs 15:9

*N*10. Jeremiah 23:23, 24

Fill in the blank after the verse with one of the ten attributes: Omniscience, Omnipotence, Omnipresence, Eternity, Holiness, Righteousness, Faithfulness, Mercy and Loving-kindness, and Love. (Choices may be used more than once)

1. Nehemiah 9:7, 8

Righteousness

2. 2 Peter 3:9

Mercy and Loving-kindness

3. Proverbs 15:3

Omniscience

4. Psalm 139:7-12

Omnipresence

5. James 1:17

Eternity

6. Isaiah 57:15

Holiness

7. 2 Timothy4:8

Righteousness

8. Daniel 4:35

Omnipotence

9. Exodus 3:14

Eternity

10. 1 John 4:8-16

Love

The Doctrine of Jesus Christ

THE DOCTRINE OF JESUS CHRIST.

A. THE PERSON OF CHRIST.

I. THE HUMANITY OF JESUS CHRIST.

1. HE HAD A HUMAN PARENTAGE.

2. HE GREW AS OTHER HUMAN BEINGS DO.

3. HE HAD THE APPEARANCE OF A MAN.

4. HE WAS POSSESSED OF A BODY, SOUL, AND SPIRIT.

5. HE WAS SUBJECT TO THE SINLESS INFIRMITIES OF HUMANITY.

6. HUMAN NAMES ARE GIVEN TO HIM.

II. THE DEITY OF JESUS CHRIST.

1. DIVINE NAMES ARE GIVEN TO HIM.

2. DIVINE WORSHIP IS ASCRIBED TO HIM.

3. DIVINE QUALITIES AND PROPERTIES ARE POSSESSED BY HIM.

4. DIVINE OFFICES ARE ASCRIBED TO HIM.

5. DIVINE ATTRIBUTES ARE POSSESSED BY HIM.

6. CHRIST'S NAME IS COUPLED WITH THAT OF THE FATHER.

7. THE SELF-CONSCIOUSNESS OF JESUS CHRISTAS MANIFESTED:

a) In His Visit to the Temple.

b) In His Baptism.

c) In His Temptation.

d) In the Calling of the Twelve and the Seventy.

e) In the Sermon on the Mount.

B. THE WORK OF CHRIST.

1. HIS DEATH.

2. HIS RESURRECTION.

3. HIS ASCENSION AND EXALTATION.

Painting of the Virgin Mary

The opening statements about the Name and personality and Jesus Christ being essential to Christianity may seem obvious. However, the other religions mentioned depend on teachings of a human prophet giving advice and his own opinions presented in obscure and confusing ways. Jesus Christ stated that He was God and that He gave eternal life by His own death, burial and resurrection.

Note that the omission of reference to the Virgin Birth in Mark, John, and the works of Paul is fairly well explained, but the quote by L.F. Anderson is nothing but heresy. The Virgin Birth is not a "marvelous tale" or a "gospel tradition." It is truth, recorded in its proper chronological place in Matthew and Luke. "Tradition," even in the lifetime of Christ, falsely said that Jesus was either the son of Joseph or illegitimate.

True or False

*T*1. Jesus came from Abraham, David, and Mary.

*F*2. The early church did not emphasize Jesus' virgin birth.

*T*3. Jesus' growth in wisdom, stature, and favor with God and man were a result of both His human nurture and divine nature.

*F*4. Jesus gave up some of His divine nature to become a man.

*F*5. Incarnated is the same as carnal.

Matching

Match the letter of the divine name by which Christ is called to the number of the verse. Choices will be used more than once, and more than one letter choice may be possible.

A. Lord B. The First and the Last C. Only Begotten D. Son of God E. God F. The Alpha and Omega

E 1. Tit. 2:13

C 2. John 1:18

D,E 3. 1 John 5:20

A 4. Acts 16:31

D,E 5. Hebrews 1:8

A 6. Matt. 22:43-45

D 7. Matt. 16:16

A 8. Acts 4:33

D 9. Luke 1:35

D 10. Matt. 27:43

B 11. Isaiah 41:4

F 12. Revelation 22:13

D 13. John 5:25

C 14. John 1:14

D 15. Mark 1:1

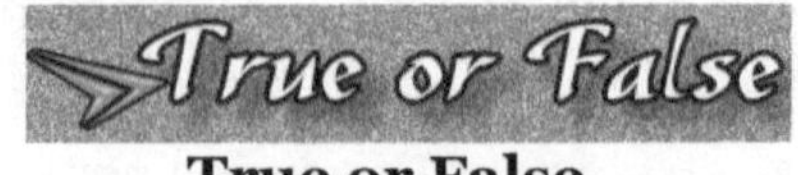

True or False

F 1. Jesus Christ reacted to worship the same way Peter and the angels who appeared to men did.

T 2. Herod died because he accepted worship.

F 3. No one tried to worship an apostle.

T 4. Jesus' attitude toward worship of Him disproves some people's idea that He was only a "good teacher" and "good example."

T 5. God commands that men and angels worship God.

Under "HE POSSESSES THE QUALITIES AND PROPERTIES OF DEITY," Evans combines the qualities of Self-Existence and Life-Giving Power. There doesn't seem to be any reason for doing this. They have therefore been separated as choices below.

Multiple Choice

Multiple Choice

Write the letter of the quality or property of Deity in the blank in front of the number of the matching verse below.

A. Pre-existence B. Self-Existence C. Life-Giving Power D. Immutability (unchanging) E. Fullness of the Godhead

C 1. John 1:4

B 2. Hebrews 7:16

A 3. John 1:1

E 4. Colossians 2:9

A 5. John 17:5

A 6. Colossians 1:15-17

C 7. John 5:21

B 8. John 5:26

C 9. John 17:3

B 10. John 17:5

D 11. Hebrews 13:8

A 12. John 8:58

C 13. John 14:6

D 14. Hebrews 1:12

A 15. John 1:1

True or False

T 1. John 1 teaches that Creation demonstrates the mind and might of Jesus Christ.

F 2. Hebrews 1:10 shows that the Creation has dignity.

F 3. Revelation 3:14 and Colossians 1:15 show that Jesus Christ began with Creation.

F 4. Colossians 1:16-18 proves three things: Jesus Christ is 1. Creator, 2. Head of the Church, 3. Preeminent among the Dead.

F 5. According to Hebrews 1:3, God has upheld all things for His Son.

T 6. One example of blasphemy is a human claiming divine power.

T 7. The parable of the two debtors (Luke 7:41-43) illustrates the deity of Jesus Christ.

F 8. Only Elisha raised the dead in the same way that Jesus Christ did.

F 9. Jesus Christ died to give God the power to judge men.

F 10. In John 6:39 ff (the people misunderstand the Bread of Life) and John 11:25 (Jesus comes to the tomb of Lazarus), Jesus declares His power to raise the dead six times.

Matching

Match the letter of each of the following divine attributes with the number of Evans' explanation of how it was manifested in Jesus Christ. (Note that Evans points out that Mark 13:32 "But of that day and that hour knoweth no man, no, not the angels which are in heaven, neither the Son, but the Father" seems to put a limitation on

Christ's Omniscience, but he offers some of the accepted conservative explanations for this.)

A. Omnipotence B. Omniscience C. Omnipresence

B 1. prophesying events as if present at them rather than remote in time

A 2. raising the dead

C 3. " ... the church, Which is his body, the fullness of him that filleth all in all."

A 4. turning water into wine

B 5. knowing the thoughts of the disciples

C 6. "... and, lo, I am with you alway, even unto the end of the world."

B 7. confirmation of Mosaic authorship of the Pentateuch

C 8. "For where two or three are gathered together in my name, there am I in the midst of them."

A 9. healing disease

C 10. "... sanctified in Christ Jesus, called to be saints, with all that in every place call upon the name of Jesus Christ our Lord ..."

True or False

T 1. The name of Jesus Christ appears together with God the Father's as the bestower of Grace.

F 2. The baptismal formula says, "In the names of the Father, and of the Son, and of the Holy Ghost."

T 3. John 17:3 says that life eternal is knowing the Father and the Son.

T 4. Both God and Jesus Christ are equally able to give comfort.

F 5. The repeated use of a plural verb in the passages mentioning both God and Jesus Christ proves that God and Jesus Christ are equal.

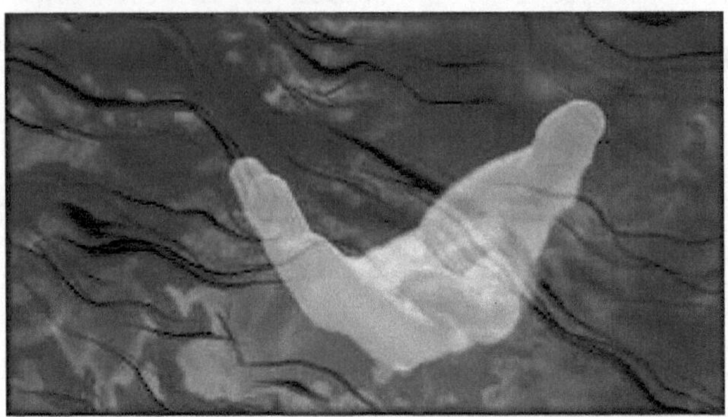

Abstract hand image

(Note that there may be some confusion in the study of the section entitled "7. THE SELF-CONSCIOUSNESS OF JESUS REGARDING HIS OWN PERSON AND WORK." Evans might seem to some to be saying that Jesus gradually became conscious of His position as God's Son and not Joseph's, and grew in that consciousness. However, he makes clear that he is building a case for the opposite position. From Jesus' first recorded speech, through all the events listed, Jesus asserts His Sonship with clarity. His human Jewish education included memorizing much of the Old Testament and he used that knowledge, and the knowledge that his audience knew these Scriptures too, to solidify in the minds of his Disciples and everyone He taught that He was the fulfillment of the teaching. Each incident is not a stage of enlightenment for Him but a revealing to man of the true nature of the Son of God grounded in the Word of God.

True or False

T 6. No one else in the Scriptures but Jesus Christ refers to God as "My Father."

T 7. Jesus never referred to Joseph in the Scriptures as "my father."

F 8. Jesus was not familiar with the ministry of John the Baptist before His baptism.

T 9. John did not fully understand the purpose Jesus Christ had on Earth, at least up until the time of his (John's) imprisonment by Herod.

F 10. The baptism of Christ fulfilled an Old Testament prophecy in Jeremiah.

Ary Scheffer - Temptation of Christ (1854)

Evans seems to be stretching a point in the section "c) As Set Forth in the Record of the Temptation." It's true that Satan wanted to get Jesus to skip steps and get to a quick, earthly establishment of the kingdom. It's also clear that Christ was conscious of His position, true nature, and His plan and purpose, based on His responses to the temptation. Still, it's difficult to understand why Evans thinks speculating on what knowledge the Devil did or didn't have strengthens his case. It is demonstrated throughout the Scriptures that Satan knows the Scriptures but does not believe or probably even fully understand them, takes wrong actions because of his willfully incomplete or wrong understanding, and is in all ways a poor "witness" to Christ's self-knowledge.

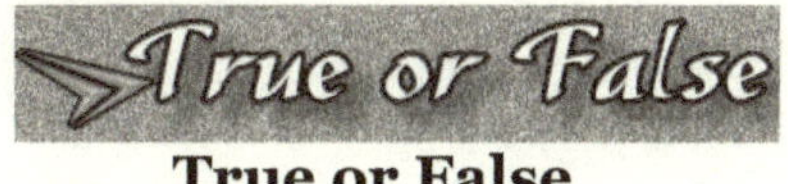

True or False

F 11. Satan's purpose was to get Jesus to acknowledge that He was the Ideal King.

T 12. Jesus' choosing of twelve disciples indicates His knowledge of the future.

T 13. Rejecting the message of Christ is the same as rejecting the Father.

T 14. Fidelity to Jesus is that on which the final destiny of men depends.

T 15. Christ set himself above the Law of Moses.

T 16. Christianity is meaningless without the atonement.

F 17. Christianity can be ethical without the death and resurrection of Christ.

T 18. The incarnation and the atonement can neither be separated nor put in order of greater or lesser importance.

F 19. Evans says that one out of every fifty verses in the New Testament deals with redemption.

T 20. There are, according to Evans, 175 mentions of the death of Christ in the New Testament.

Multiple Choice

Multiple Choice

Identify the source of the following numbered Scripture quotes by circling the letter of the correct choice below.

A. Jesus Christ B. OT Writings of Moses C. OT prophets/prophetesses D. NT Mount of Transfiguration (or referring to that event) E. Early NT Witnesses (e.g., Zacharias, Mary, Simeon, Anna)

C 1. "Seventy weeks are determined ... to finish the transgression, and to make an end of sins, and to make reconciliation for iniquity, and to bring in everlasting righteousness ... And after threescore and two weeks shall Messiah be cut off, but not for himself."

E 2. "For mine eyes have seen thy salvation, Which thou hast prepared before the face of all people; A light to lighten the Gentiles, and the glory of thy people Israel."

A 3. "O fools, and slow of heart to believe all that the prophets have spoken: Ought not Christ to have suffered these things, and to enter into his glory?"

B 4. "And I will put enmity between thee and the woman, and between thy seed and her seed; it shall bruise thy head, and thou shalt bruise his heel."

E 5. "And she coming in that instant gave thanks likewise unto the Lord, and spake of him to all them that looked for redemption in Jerusalem."

C 6. "But he was wounded for our transgressions, he was bruised for our iniquities: the chastisement of our peace was upon him; and with his stripes we are healed."

C 7. "For I know that my redeemer liveth, and that he shall stand at the latter day upon the earth: And though after my skin worms destroy this body, yet in my flesh shall I see God."

E 8. "Blessed be the Lord God of Israel; for he hath visited and redeemed his people, And hath raised up an horn of salvation for us in the house of his servant David."

C 9. "My heart rejoiceth in the LORD, mine horn is exalted in the LORD: my mouth is enlarged over mine enemies; because I rejoice in thy salvation."

E 10. "My soul doth magnify the Lord, And my spirit hath rejoiced in God my Saviour."

D 11. "Who appeared in glory, and spake of his decease which he should accomplish at Jerusalem. "

A 12. "And they shall scourge him, and put him to death: and the third day he shall rise again."

C 13. "I gave My back to those who struck Me, and My cheeks to those who plucked out the beard. I did not hide My face from shame and spitting."

D 14. "And we beheld his glory, the glory as of the only begotten of the Father, full of grace and truth."

A 15. "And said unto them, 'Thus it is written, and thus it behooved Christ to suffer, and to rise from the dead the third day.'"

C 16. "And I will pour on the house of David and on the inhabitants of Jerusalem the Spirit of grace and supplication, then they will look on Me whom they pierced. Yes, they will mourn for Him as one mourns for his only son, and grieve for Him as one grieves for a firstborn."

D 17. "We made known unto you the power and coming of our Lord Jesus Christ, but were eyewitnesses of his majesty. For he received from God the Father honour and glory, when there came such a voice to him from the excellent glory, This is my beloved Son, in whom I am well pleased."

C 18. "And he saw that there was no man, and wondered that there was no intercessor: therefore his arm brought salvation unto him; and his righteousness, it sustained him."

A 19. "And as Moses lifted up the serpent in the wilderness, even so must the Son of man be lifted up: That whosoever believeth in him should not perish, but have eternal life:"

C 20. "For thou wilt not leave my soul in hell; neither wilt thou suffer thine Holy One to see corruption."

Matching

Match the letter of the correct aspect of the death of Christ with the numbered verses below.

A. Ransom B. Propitiation C. Reconciliation D. Substitution

D 1. 1 Peter 2:24

C 2. Romans 5:10

A 3. 1 Peter l:18

D 4. II Corinthians 5:21

B 5. Romans 3:25

D 6. Isaiah 53:6

A 7. I Timothy 2:6

D 8. I Peter 3:18

B 9. Hebrews 2:17

C 10. II Corinthians 5:18, 19

B 11. I John 2:2

C 12. Colossians 1:20

A 13. Matthew 20:28

C 14. Ephesians 2:16

A 15. Galatians 3:13

Match the correct letter of one of the four aspects with the numbered examples below. (Note that an example is not the same as a synonym. These are not necessarily perfect illustrations, just examples.)

A. Ransom B. Propitiation C. Reconciliation D. Substitution

C 1. break down barrier

B 2. covering

A 3. buy back a captive

B 4. pardoning

D 5. Archelaus succeeding Herod

B 6. overlooking

A 7. paying a price

C 8. remove enmity

D 9. ram for Isaac

C 10. change attitude

A 11. commute a death sentence

C 12. create friendship

D 13. Passover lamb

A 14. free a prisoner

D 15. fish for serpent

A 16. purchase a slave

D 17. Christ for Barabbas

Identify the views of Christ's death below by marking U for Unscriptural or I for incomplete. (Evans lists all as unscriptural, but it is possible to make the distinction that Christ's death did accomplish other purposes which were not the primary ones.)

U 1. Martyrdom

U 2. Accident

I 3. Love

I 4. Example of suffering

U 5. Example of God's justice

Fill in the Blank

(Note that Evans refers to the passages below in the discussion of the Martyrdom Theory, but the references for the verses are not in the text. He very rightly points out some uncomfortable truths about the martyrdom position.)

Learn how Jesus Christ's death is a "Mystery" according to Paul by answering these questions based on I Corinthians 2.

1. Paul first says that he declared the of God.
testimony

2. In a courtroom giving evidence helps people find out what might be hidden and understand .
truth

3. Paul wanted to consider only one piece of evidence, Jesus Christ, and Him .
Crucified

4. Paul's speech was a demonstration of the and of power (in other words, to demonstrate God's power to teach us and give understanding).
Spirit

5. When Paul says he speaks God's wisdom in a mystery, he explains that it is hard to understand because God ordained it before the for our glory, meaning that He

made a plan for our great good.
World

6. Paul mentions a group of people, calling them the (blank) and probably referring to mortal men and Satan himself.
The princes of this world

7. The mystery, if these people had understood it, would have changed a course of action they took. What was that action?
They would not have crucified the Lord of Glory.

8. The mystery Paul speaks of cannot be understood by the of man, but only through the of God.
spirit, Spirit

9. The "solution" to the mystery is given to us by the answer to the second part of question 8.
freely

10. The key to understanding the mystery is to compare things with , that is, to look at the Scripture and its teaching as opposed to relying on man's flawed and sinful "reasoning.".
spiritual, spiritual

11. Compare Matthew 27:46 to Acts 7:55-56. was missing at the death of Christ but was present at the death of Stephen.
God

12. According to Matthew 26:39 and Luke 22: 39-46, did Christ face His death with joy and song like many recorded martyrdoms? Can you give at least one reason why or why not?
No. Two possible reasons are: 1. The knowledge He would be separated from God; and 2. That He would bear the sins of the world.

13. According to I Corinthians 15:1-4, Paul says the three parts of the Gospel are the , , and of Jesus Christ.
death, burial, resurrection

14. The ultimate difference between the death of Jesus Christ and that of any martyr, according to Evans, is that Paul preached not through the death of Stephen, but through the death of Christ.
forgiveness

True or False

T 1. If God had only wanted an example of His governmental justice, He had no need for Jesus Christ to die.

F 2. The love theory is flawed because love can only cover sins, not atone for them.

T 3. According to Evans, atonement is necessary to God's holiness because of His close connection to mankind.

F 4. The examples in the Old Testament of laws and prohibitions only applied to worship.

F 5. We have no parallel examples of visual or physical reminders in our culture today.

F 6. The OT law is irrelevant because it is just legalism today.

T 7. Jesus Christ fulfilled prophecy to reinforce the authority of the Scriptures.

T 8. The New Testament writers repeat the phrase "that the Scriptures might be fulfilled" (or something similar) to establish the authority of Scriptures.

T 9. The following verses support universal atonement: Isa. 53:6; 1 Tim. 2:6; 1 John 2:2.

T 10. Verses Evans gives as supporting limited atonement rely on assumptions such as a shepherd only having a limited number of sheep, not all the sheep in the world.

T 11. "The atonement is sufficient for all; it is efficient for those who believe in Christ."

F 12. Evans gives Scriptures supporting the view that the atonement is for individuals but not for the world in general.

T 13. Evans states that Hebrews 12:9 means the same thing as the quote "if the whole universe of captives would believe in the Redeemer, no chain of the devil could hold them."

T 14. The illustrations Evans uses of the Greeks, the Romans and the Jews make the point that many groups limit salvation to those who follow the works their culture considers important.

T 15. Romans 5:6-10 and I Peter 3:18 make the same point.

F 16. Paul is not a good example of one whom Christ died to save.

T 17. Evans makes the point that the real essence of the limited atonement theory is that Christ died for the Church.

F 18. Martin Luther never taught that atonement was for the individual.

T 19. Christ allows for weakness even in the belief in His atonement.

T 20. Revelation 7:9-15 demonstrates the scope of salvation.

F 21. The Fall of Man had only a spiritual effect on the Universe.

T 22. The death of Christ reconciled things in heaven to God.

F 23. Colossians 1:20 is talking only about the future.

T 24. II Peter 3:13 is talking only about the future.

F 25. Hebrews 9:23 is talking only about the future.

Matching

Matching

Write the letter of the effect of Christ's death on the world of men next to the number of the Scripture verse that matches

A. Enmity between God and Man Removed B. Propitiation for the World's Sin Provided C. Satan's Power over Man Neutralized D. Question of the World's Sin Settled E. Claims of a Broken Law and Curse on Man Removed F. Justification G. Adoption H. Sanctification I. Access to God J. Inheritance K. Removal of All Fear of Death

G 1. Galatians 4:3-5

D 2. Hebrews 9:26

H 3. Hebrews 10:10

A 4. Romans 5:10

B 5. I John 2:2

K 6. Hebrews 2:14,15

B 7. John 4:10

C 8. John 12:31,32

E 9. Colossians 2:14

C 10. Colossians 2:10

D 11. Romans 3:25, 26

A 12. Colossians 1:20-22

E 13. Galatians 3:13

F 14. Romans 5:9

I 15. Hebrews 10:19, 20

C 16. John 16:9, 10

J 17. Hebrews 9:15

True or False

T 1. Believers and unbelievers agree on the importance of the resurrection to Christianity.

F 2. Only preaching, not faith, is vain without the resurrection.

F 3. Christ didn't need to rise from the dead to confirm the forgiveness of sins.

F 4. The resurrection is spoken of in the New Testament 200 times.

T 5. If the resurrection is not true there is no basis for believing or practicing Christianity.

Matching

Write the letter of the arguments for and against the resurrection in the blank next to the number of evidence that best matches it. (Choices may be used more than once.)

A. "Swoon Theory" (Jesus did not die but only passed out and revived in the tomb) B. Spiritual Resurrection Theory C. Differences in Christ's Body (Christ's resurrected body differed significantly from his mortal body) D. Testimony of Witnesses E. Contradictions or Discrepancies in the Accounts

A 1. The resurrected Christ was active and healthy.

B 2. The body was laid in the tomb and disappeared from the tomb.

A 3. Separation of water from blood indicates death.

A 4. The soldiers did not break His legs on the cross, because they had confirmed that He was dead.

C 5. Christ's resurrected body was no longer subject to death.

A 6. Jesus Christ testified that He had been dead.

B 7. Soldiers were bribed to say that the body had been stolen.

(Note the Religious leaders planned for this defense ahead of time by saying they wanted a guard to prevent theft.)

B 8. The linen wrappings remained neatly in the tomb.

(Contrast this with the resurrection of Lazarus, where he came forth bound hand and foot in grave clothes and had to be set free.)

A 9. Pilate at first disbelieved that he could already be dead and demanded confirmation.

B 10. Angels (seen by soldiers and followers) testified that Jesus had predicted His resurrection and testified that it had occurred.

A 11. Joseph of Arimathea would not have buried Christ if He had not been officially pronounced dead.

B 12. The disciples recognized in the resurrected Christ the body that had been dead, down to voice, mannerisms and the nail prints and wounded side (except in circumstances where God's intervention or unbelief may have delayed recognition, as with Mary in the Garden or the disciples on the road to Emmaus.)

A 13. Both Joseph and the women had oils and spices prepared to anoint His dead body.

B 14. The disciples witnessed the physical evidences of the resurrection.

C 15. Christ could pass through doors, vanish out of sight, and could rise up into the heavens.

E 16. "Contradictions" in the accounts of the resurrection result from incomplete study of the events.

D 17. Over 500 people witnessed Christ's resurrection.

D 18. Tertullian, a Church father, wrote that Pontius Pilate reported the resurrection to the Roman senate.

E 19. "Discrepancies" in the accounts result from failure to order the gospel events correctly

D 20. "They (the disciples, apostles and New Testament witnesses to Christ) have been the unrivalled pattern of all mature and moral manhood for nearly two thousand years."

Alexander Ivanov Appearance of Christ to Mary Magdalene, 1835

Note: Evans' arguments from Cause and Effect are either difficult to understand or obvious. Two points discussed below are worth noting. The Sabbath remains the

Sabbath. Jews who believed in Christ did observe the Lord's Day and worship then, but it did not "become" the Sabbath, which remained a separate day. It has become conventional to Gentile Christians to refer to Sunday as the Sabbath but this is not part of the New Testament teaching. Evans makes a very good point that the Christian faith is founded on the Resurrection, not the life or teachings of Christ. The disciples were discouraged, fearful, in hiding, going back to their former occupations until Christ convinced them of the reality that He arose.

True or False

F 1. The resurrection is not a testimony to the deity of Christ.

T 2. The resurrection is the basis for the authority of Christ's teachings.

T 3. The priests exiting the temple after the sacrifice is a picture of the resurrection.

F 4. An intercessor is still needed because we need daily forgiveness, Satan's accusations need to be answered, and only Christ's prayers are heard.

F 5. The Old Testament measurement of God's power is the Exodus. The New Testament measurement is the Second Coming.

T 6. Jesus' resurrection provides assurance of our resurrection.

F 7. The example of I Corinthians 15:22 is a spiritual resurrection.

T 8. The resurrection is an assurance of final judgment.

F 9. The Ascension of Christ means His being given a place of power at the right hand of God.

F 10. Acts 1:9-11 records the Exaltation of Christ.

Matching

Matching

Write A for Ascension or B for Exaltation beside the number of the verse it matches. (In some verses both answers may apply)

B 1. Psalm 110:1

B 2. Philippians 2:9

A 3. Acts 1:9-11

B 4. Ephesians 1:20,21

B 5. Hebrews 1:3

A,B 6. Psalm 68:18

A 7. Luke 9:51

A 8. John 6:62

A 9. John 20:17

A 10. Mark 16:19

A 11. Luke 24:51

A 12. John 3:13

A,B 13. Ephesians 4:8-10

B 14. Hebrews 10:12

B 15. Acts 7:55, 56 (Note that There is a Typo in the e-text of Evans, listing this second verse as 36)

B 16. Acts 2:33, 34

B 17. Acts 5:31

A,B 18. I Peter 3:22

A,B 19. Hebrews 4:14

A,B 20 I Timothy 3:16

Evans' comments on the necessity of the ascension and exaltation of Christ are more examples of his opinions, some of which have a biblical basis, though he presents no Scriptures in support of them except general references to events in the Bible.

Multiple Choice

Multiple Choice

Place the letter of the correct aspect or result of the ascension and exaltation next to the verse that matches it.

A. Bodily and Visible B. Passing through the Heavens C. Take His place at the Father's right hand D. Entered heaven as a forerunner E. Gone to prepare a place for His people F. Appearing before God for us G. "Fill all things" (be present everywhere) and await universal dominion H. Confident access into God's Presence I. Assurance of Immortality J. Confidence in God's providence (all things work together for good)

C 1. Revelation 12:10

A 2. Acts 1:9-11

C 3. Psalm 110:1

A 4. Luke 25:51

B 5. Hebrews 4:14

G 6. Ephesians 4:10

G 7. Hebrews 10:12, 13

B 8. Hebrews 7:26

B 9. Ephesians 6

C 10. Ephesians 1:20

C 11. Colossians 3:1

E 12. John 14:2

C 13. Colossians 2:15

C 14. Zechariah 3:1

C 15. Genesis 48:13-19

G 16. Acts 3:20,21

C 17. Psalm 110:5

D 18. Hebrews 6:20

C 19. Romans 8:34

I 20. II Corinthians 5:1-8

E 21. Hebrews 9:21-24

F 22. Hebrews 9:24

J 23. Ephesians 1:22

A 24. I Corinthians 15:51, 52

G 25. Jeremiah 23:24

B 26. Ephesians 4:10

H 27. Hebrews 4:14-16

J 28. Colossians 1:15-18

C 29. Acts 5:31

The Doctrine of the Holy Spirit

THE DOCTRINE OF THE HOLY SPIRIT

I. THE PERSONALITY OF THE HOLY SPIRIT.

1. PERSONAL NAMES GIVEN TO THE SPIRIT.

2. PERSONAL PRONOUNS USED OF THE SPIRIT.

3. THE SPIRIT ASSOCIATED WITH THE FATHER AND THE SON.

4. THE SPIRIT POSSESSES PERSONAL CHARACTERISTICS.

5. PERSONAL ACTS ARE ASCRIBED TO THE HOLY SPIRIT.

6. THE SPIRIT IS SUBJECT TO PERSONAL TREATMENT.

II. THE DEITY OF THE HOLY SPIRIT.

1. DIVINE NAMES ARE GIVEN TO THE SPIRIT.

2. DIVINE ATTRIBUTES.

3. DIVINE WORKS.

4. NAME OF THE SPIRIT ASSOCIATED WITH NAMES OF THE DEITY.

5. COMPARISON OF OLD TESTAMENT PASSAGES WITH SOME IN THE NEW

TESTAMENT.

III. THE NAMES OF THE HOLY SPIRIT.

1. THE HOLY SPIRIT.

2. THE SPIRIT OF GRACE.

3. THE SPIRIT OF BURNING.

4. THE SPIRIT OF TRUTH.

5. THE SPIRIT OF LIFE.

6. THE SPIRIT OF WISDOM AND KNOWLEDGE.

7. THE SPIRIT OF PROMISE.

8. THE SPIRIT OF GLORY.

9. THE SPIRIT OF GOD AND OF CHRIST.

IV. THE WORK OF THE HOLY SPIRIT.

1. IN RELATION TO THE WORLD.

a) The Universe.

b) The World of Mankind.

2. IN RELATION TO THE BELIEVER.

3. IN RELATION TO THE SCRIPTURES.

4. IN RELATION TO JESUS CHRIST.

V. OFFENCES AGAINST THE HOLY SPIRIT.

1. BY THE SINNER.

a) Resisting.

b) Insulting.

c) Blaspheming.

2. BY THE BELIEVER.

a) Grieving.

b) Lying to.

c) Quenching.

True or False

F 1. According to Evans, the OT period is the period of the Father, the Gospel period is the period of the Son, and the period from Pentecost to the Second Coming is the period of the Church

T 2. “Now concerning spiritual gifts” might be better translated “matters pertaining to the Spirit.”

T 3. One of the verses describing sin against the Holy Spirit as grievous is Ephesians 4:30.

T 4. John 14:17 is one verse that describes the personal relationship of the Holy Spirit to believers.

F 5. Names and symbols for the Holy Spirit include breath, wind, power, oil (KJV unction, an anointing with oil), fire, water, and iron.

T 6. One of the reasons people think of the Holy Spirit as impersonal is the use of concepts like laying on hands, anointing and breathing to receive the Spirit.

T 7. The Apostles do not usually mention the Holy Spirit in connection with blessings or salutations.

F 8. The Word used for spirit is masculine.

F 9. The word Comforter used for the Holy Spirit in John 14:16 is the same as that used for Jesus Christ in John 16:7.

T 10. Jesus uses a masculine definite article for the Comforter.

T 11. The baptismal formula not only supports the Trinity but the personality of the Holy Spirit.

F 12. II Corinthians 13:14 is the reference for the baptismal formula.

T 13. Apostles make frequent reference to the Holy Spirit in ways that would make it contradictory to use an impersonal noun in reference to Him.

T 14. Some acts of the Holy Spirit (such as intercession) are also attributed to Christ.

F 15. It is not possible to lie to the Holy Spirit.

Multiple Choice

Multiple Choice

Write the letter of the best choice next to the number. More than one answer may be correct.

D 1. The Scripture passage where the Holy Spirit is compared to the wind is

A. 1 John 2:20 B. Acts 2:1-4 C. John 20:22 D. John 3:5-8

B 2. The Scripture passage where the Holy Spirit's presence is described using fire as a symbol is

A. 1 John 2:20 B. Acts 2:1-4 C. John 20:22 D. John 3:5-8

C 3. The Scripture passage where the Holy Spirit's presence is described using breath as a symbol is

A. 1 John 2:20 B. Acts 2:1-4 C. John 20:22 D. John 3:5-8

B 4. . The Scripture passage where the Holy Spirit's presence is described using oil (KJV unction, an anointing) as a symbol is

A. Acts 2:1-4 B. 1 John 2:20 C. John 20:22 D. John 3:5-8

D 5. The word Paraclete means

A. Called alongside B. Lawyer C. Comforter D. All of the above

D 6. The Holy Spirit is called the Comforter in all of the following verses except

A. John 14:16 B. John 16:7 C. John 14:26 D. I John 2:1

A 7. Which reference contains the baptismal formula?

A. Matthew 28:29 B. II Corinthians 13:14 C. Acts 15:38 D. Romans 15:13

B 8. Which verse contains the apostolic benediction?

A. Matthew 28:29 B. II Corinthians 13:14 C. Acts 15:38 D. Romans 15:13

A-D 9. Which verse(s) contains references to the Holy Spirit as directly identified with Christians?

A. Acts 10:38 B. Acts 15:38 C. Romans 15:13 D. Luke 4:14

A 10. Which personal characteristic of the Holy Spirit is supported by 1 Corinthians 2:10-11?

A. Knowledge of God and His workings B. Distribution of spiritual gifts C. The Spirit has purpose, thought, and determination. D. All of the above

C 11. Which personal act of the Holy Spirit is supported by Acts 13:2?

A. Speaking B. Making Intercession C. Calling Missionaries D. Overseeing the Church

B 12. Which personal act of the Holy Spirit is supported by Romans 8:26?

A. Speaking B. Making Intercession C. Calling Missionaries D. Overseeing the Church

A 13. Which personal act of the Holy Spirit is supported by Revelation 2:7?

A. Speaking B. Making Intercession C. Calling Missionaries D. Overseeing the Church

D 14. Which personal act of the Holy Spirit does Acts 16:6,7 support?

A. Speaking B. Making Intercession C. Calling Missionaries D. Overseeing the Church

C 15. Which personal act of the Holy Spirit is supported by Acts 20:28?

A. Speaking B. Making Intercession C. Commanding the practices of the apostles and church D. Overseeing the Church

True or False

F 1. The Holy Spirit can be grieved according to Hebrews 10:29.

F 2. The Holy Spirit can be insulted according to Ephesians 4:30.

T 3. The Holy Spirit can be blasphemed and sinned against according to Matthew 12:31,32.

F 4. The Holy Spirit can be lied to according to Acts 5:3.

T 5. The Holy Spirit can be grieved according to Ephesians 4:30.

Matching

Write A in front of the number of the verse that describes the Holy Spirit's divine attributes. Write B in front of the verse that describes the Holy Spirit's divine works.

B 1. John 3:5-8

A 2. Hebrews 9:14

B 3. Genesis 1:2

B 4. Job 33:4

A 5. Luke 1:35

B 6. Psalm 104:30

A 7. I Corinthians 2:10, 11

B 8. Romans 8:11

A 9. Psalm 139:7-10

True or False

T 1. In Acts 5, the case of Ananias lying about his land sale supports the position that the Holy Spirit is God.

T 2. II Corinthians 3:18 states that the Holy Spirit shares the name of Lord.

T 3. Hebrews 9:14 supports the position that the Holy Spirit is eternal.

F 4. Psalm 139:7-10 supports the position that the Holy Spirit is omniscient.

F 5. Luke 1:35 supports the position that the Holy Spirit is omnipresent.

T 6. I Corinthians 2:10,11 supports the position that the Holy Spirit is omniscient.

F 7. Genesis 1:2, Psalm 104:30, and Job 33:4 all support the position that the Holy Spirit is active in Regeneration.

T 8. John 3:5-8 supports the position that the Holy Spirit is active in Regeneration.

F 9. Romans 8:11 supports the position that the Holy Spirit was active in Creation.

F 10. Isaiah 6:8-10 can be compared with Hebrews 3:7-9 to show that the Old Testament passages referring to God are quoted in the New Testament as referring to the Holy Spirit.

Matching

Match the letter of the name of the Holy Spirit with the number of the verse where it occurs.

A. The Holy Spirit B. The Spirit of Grace C. The Spirit of Burning D. The Spirit of Truth E. The Spirit of Life F. The Spirit of Wisdom and Knowledge G. The Spirit of Promise H. The Spirit of Glory I. The Spirit of the Lord, of God and of Christ J. The Comforter

D 1. I John 5:6

A 2. Luke 11:13

E 3. Romans 8:2

B 4. Hebrews 10:29

C 5. Matthew 3:11,12

C 6. Isaiah 4:4

D 7. John 14:17

A 8. Romans 1:4

I 9. I Corinthians 3:16

D 10. John 15:26

H 11. I Peter 4:14

D 12. John 16:13

F 13. Isaiah 11:2

F 14. Isaiah 61:1,2

D 15. I John 4: 6

*G*16. Ephesians 1:13

J 18. John 14:16

I 19. Luke 4:28

J 20. John 16:7

True or False

T 1. There is a sense in which the creation of the universe may be ascribed to God's Spirit.

F 2. According to Isaiah 40:7, The Holy Spirit is not an agency in the preservation of nature.

F 3. John 16:8-11 includes four facts about the Holy Spirit's relationship to humanity.

F 4. The only way the Holy Spirit can bear witness of the truth of Christ is through believers.

T 5. We are "begotten of the Holy Ghost." (Although it is probably not correct to say, as Evans does, that this is the same as Jesus Christ being begotten of the Holy Ghost.)

F 6. Acts 19:2, according to Evans, is an exception to the rule that the Holy Spirit indwells believers.

F 7. To say that the Holy Spirit seals the believer means that he is protected from Satan's attacks.

T 8. Filling with the Holy Spirit can happen repeatedly.

T 9. The contrast between chapters 7 and 8 of Romans is due to the victorious life possible through the Holy Spirit.

T 10. Neither sinless perfection nor sinless imperfection are scriptural doctrines according to Evans.

F 11. Evans divides the fruits of the Spirit in Galatians 5:22,23 into two groups: Those related to God, and those related to others.

F 12. Evans quotes Psalm 37:32 as an illustration of the Spirit's guidance in man's everyday life.

T 13. Some things cannot be learned without the Holy Spirit's teaching.

T 14. The wheels within wheels described in Ezekiel is a picture of how man can be empowered by God's Spirit, according to Evans.

T 15. Psalm 56:12 is an example of the anointing of The Holy Spirit.

T 16. The Holy Spirit is the author of the Scriptures.

F 17. I Cor. 2:9-14 says that the Holy Spirit is "the Spirit of wisdom and revelation."

Matching

Match the letter of the part the Holy Spirit played in the life of Christ with the number of the correct Scripture reference. (Answers may be used more than once)

A. Christ Conceived by the Spirit B. Christ was led by the Spirit C. Christ was anointed for service D. Christ was crucified in the power of the Spirit E. Raised by the power of the Spirit F. Christ commanded the disciples and the church through the Spirit G. Christ bestowed the Holy Spirit on believers

C 1. Acts 10:38

B 2. Matt. 4:1

D 3. Heb. 9:14

E 4. Rom. 1:4

G 5. Acts 2:33

E 6. Romans 8:11

F 7. Acts 1:2

A 8. Luke 1:35

Write A next to the number of the correct answer if it deals with an offence against the Holy Spirit committed by an unbeliever and B next to the number of the correct answer if it deals with an offence against the Holy Spirit committed by a believer. (Evans' comment that there can be overlap in these areas is true, but for the purposes of this review answer according to the way they are organized in his material.)

B 1. Acts 5:3,4

A 2. Acts 6:10

A 3. Acts 7:51-57

B 4. Isaiah 63:10

A 5. Matthew 12:31,32

B 6. Ephesians 4:30, 31

B 7. II Kings 5:20-27

A 8. Hebrews 10:29

B 9. Isaiah 63:10

A 10. Acts 7:51

B 11. Galatians 5:17-19

A 12. Luke 18:32

B 13. I Thessalonians 5:19

The Doctrine of Man

THE DOCTRINE OF MAN

I. THE CREATION AND ORIGINAL CONDITION OF MAN.

1. IMAGE AND LIKENESS OF GOD.

2. PHYSICAL--MENTAL--MORAL--SPIRITUAL.

II. THE FALL OF MAN.

1. THE SCRIPTURAL ACCOUNT.

2. VARIOUS INTERPRETATIONS.

3. THE NATURE OF THE FALL.

4. THE RESULTS OF THE FALL.

a) On Adam, and Eve.

b) On the Race.

(1) Various Theories.

(2) Scriptural Declarations.

True or False

T 1. Both Genesis 1:26 and 9:6 state that God made man in His own image.

T 2. Ephesians 4:24 does not talk about the original creation of man in God's image.

F 3. Colossians 3:10 says that the new man is renewed in body after God's image.

T 4. James 3:9 gives cursing God's image as an example of the uncontrollable nature of the tongue.

F 5. Swedenborg had a correct view of God.

F 6. In Deuteronomy 4:15 Moses warned the Israelites that they had seen God's true form so did not need idols.

F 7. Psalm 17:15 and Numbers 12:8 imply that we must be sanctified to see God's true form.

F 8. Genesis 2:19-20 says that God taught Adam to speak.

T 9. Genesis 3 and Matthew 4 are parallel passages.

F 10. Judaism and Christianity are the only religions containing the fall of man.

The exalted nature and holiness of the true God, as opposed to supreme beings in other religions is an excellent point to emphasize, as Evans does. But Evans repeatedly makes the point that the fallen state of man is an obvious fact even without the account of Genesis 3. It is unclear why he does this. There is no need to reason out the fact that man is fallen from observation or experience. In fact, man delights to reason away every responsibility for his sin and corruption, and God had to clearly spell out his responsibility for him in Genesis 3.

People still try to blame God for the existence of sin, and Evans comes disturbingly close to doing that, when he says, "It is when men consider the very high character of God as set forth in Christianity, and then look at the doctrine of sin, that they find it hard to reconcile the fact that God, being the moral Being He is, should ever allow sin to come into the world. To some minds these two things seem incompatible."

Evans states that sin already existed at the time of the creation of man and as evidence of this says, "The existence of Satan and the chaotic condition of things in the beginning, strikingly testify." This statement appears to support the theory that God re-created the world from some chaotic previous creation which Satan had spoiled. The interpretation of Scriptures supporting this theory is a subject for disagreement among good men and this study will not take up that question. There are numerous Scripture passages making it clear that Satan rebelled against God before Adam did, so sin did indeed exist before the fall. It is also true that man in most of the Scriptures demonstrates a fallen nature, not the nature given to Him at creation when "everything was very good."

Benjamin West Expulsion from the Garden 1791

Evans, in the discussion of the effects of the fall, brings up the theory of the "age of responsibility," sometimes called the "age of accountability," a commonly held belief that children must attain a certain age, varying in different denominations, before they are held responsible or accountable for sin. That is to say, if a child dies before reaching this age he will not be held to blame for not accepting Christ's atonement. Different good scholars and historians use different proof texts and arguments from scriptural indicators to arrive at their conclusions. Others disagree that such a theory is valid. The Roman Catholic concept of "Limbo" and other heresies, including baptismal regeneration, result from attempts to explain the accountability issue in the very young, but all of this is outside the scope of this study. It is merely mentioned here in the notes to explain what Evans means by this term.

Multiple Choice

Multiple Choice

D 1. All of the following Scriptures deal with the fall except

A. Romans 3:10-23 B. Genesis 3 C. I Timothy 2:14 D. Genesis 8:21

A 2. All of the following Scriptures deal with man's fallen condition except

A. Genesis 1:26 B. Genesis 6:5 C. Psalm 14 D. I Samuel 2:17

C 3. The correct interpretation of the fall of man is

A. Folklore in poetic form B. Allegorical narrative C. Historical literal D. Tantric Mantra

D 4. Parts of the Fall Narrative that support the idea of its being non-literal are

A. Geographical detail B. Demonstrated effects of the curse C. New Testament affirmations D. None of the above

B 5. All of the following Scriptures refer to the fall except

A. I Corinthians 15:56 B. Matthew 6:13 C. Matthew 19:4 I Timothy 2:13-15

C 6. The first sin of man was all of the following except

A. deliberately overstepping Divine limit B. denial of the divine will C. unintentional accident D. positive disbelief in the word of God

A 7. The results of the fall included all of the following except

A. Confusion of language B. ground cursed C. hard physical labor D. Pain in childbirth

A 8. Secondary results of the fall included all of the following except

A. destruction of the Garden of Eden B. hiding from God's presence C. shame over sin D. fear of God

C 9. The "bad example" theory of sin's effect is false because

A. Scriptures teach redemption by works B. Pelagius proved it false C. Man demonstrates his sin nature throughout the Scriptures D. No one was affected by Adam's example

D 10. The semi-Pelagian theory states that

A. Man is destitute of original righteousness B. Adam's sin and guilt is not imputed to his descendants C. The "Dawn of Consciousness" prevents man from working out his own salvation D. Both A and B

B 11. The Augustinian theory considers all of the aspects of the sin nature except

A. sin is imputed to Adam's posterity B. the half-sick, half-well nature of man's spirit C. the organic unity of mankind D. the unity of the race in Adam

Matching

Match the letter of the aspect of the Scriptural teaching about the fall's consequences with the number of the reference. Answers may be used more than once.

A. All men regardless of condition or class are sinners B. universal sinfulness is vitally connected with Adam's sin C. the whole world rests under condemnation, wrath and curse D. unregenerate men are children of the devil, not children of God E. the whole race is helpless, captive to sin and Satan F. the mental, moral, spiritual and physical nature of man is affected by sin

D 1. I John 5:19

C 2. John 3:36

A 3. Romans 3:9,

A 4. Romans 3:10

F 5. Ephesians 4:18

A 6. Psalm 14

F 7. Genesis 6:5

A 8. Isaiah. 53:6

B 9. Romans 5:19

C 10. Romans 3:19

A 11. Romans 3:22

C 12. Galatians 3:10

F 13. II Corinthians 7:5

B 14. Romans 5:12

D 15. John 8:44

E 16. Romans 7

E 17. John 8:31-36

C 18. Ephesians 2:3

E 19. Ephesians 2:3

D 20. I John 3:8-10

F 21. I Corinthians 2:14

F 22. Jeremiah 17:9, 10

B 23. Romans 5:16

F 24. Titus 1:15

A 25. Romans 3:23

F 26. Romans 7:18

True or False

F 1. Unconverted man suffers from an entire absence of conscience according to John 8:9.

T 2. Mark 10:21 says that man is not devoid of the ability to have good qualities.

F 3. Man has very little of the love of God in him, according to John 5:42.

F 4. Romans 8:7 says that the carnal mind can deceive us into thinking it is subject to God.

T 5. Romans 7:18 and 23 say that man possesses the will to do good but is at war within himself.

The Doctrines of Salvation

THE DOCTRINES OF SALVATION

A. Repentance

A. Repentance

I. THE IMPORTANCE OF THE DOCTRINE.

II. THE NATURE OF REPENTANCE.

1. AS TOUCHING THE INTELLECT.

2. AFFECTING THE EMOTIONS.

3. WILL.

a) Confess Sin.

b) Forsake Sin.

c) Turn to God.

III. HOW REPENTANCE IS PRODUCED.

1. DIVINE SIDE.

2. HUMAN SIDE.

3. QUESTION OF MEANS.

IV. RESULTS OF REPENTANCE.

1. GODWARD.

2. MANWARD.

Short Answer

1. Name two New Testament preachers who began their public ministries with a call to repentance and list Scriptures that support this position. *Jesus Christ and John the Baptist Matthew 3:1,2; 4:17*

2. Luke 24:47 and Mark 6:12 support the fact that Jesus Christ's charge upon sending out the twelve and the seventy included preaching what? *Repentance*

3. What is the common message in the preaching of Peter and Paul, as stated in Acts 2:38 and Acts 20:21. *Repentance*

4. Based on II Peter 3:9 and Acts 17:30, God's greatest desire for man is that he do what? *Repent*

5. What is the fate of unrepentant man according to Luke 13:3? *Repent or perish*

Matching

Write the letter of one of the three aspects of the nature of repentance in front of the number of the Scripture that supports it. Also, a choice may be used more than once or apply to more than one aspect

(Note that some Scripture passages do not have the exact word "repent" or "repentance" in them, or do not relate directly to man, but the student should look for a clear statement of the meaning or concept of repentance in its various aspects to make the correct match)

A. Intellectual B. Emotional C. Will and Disposition

B 1. II Corinthians 7:9-11

A,C 2. Luke 15:18, 20

C 3. Isaiah 55:7

A 4. Acts 2:14-40

B 5. Luke 10:13

C 6. Matthew 3:8, 10

C 7. I Thessalonians 1:9

B,C 8. Psalm 38:18

C 9. Luke 15:18,20, 21

A,C 10. Luke 18:13

C 11. Matthew 5:23, 24

A 12. Matthew 21:29

C 13. Proverbs 28:13

C 14. Acts 26:18

B 15. Genesis 6:6

C 16. James 5:16

True or False

F 1. Acts 11:18 explains how repentance works differently for the Gentiles and the Jews.

T 2. Part of repentance is acknowledging the truth, according to II Timothy 2:25.

T 3. According to Acts 5:30, 31, one result of repentance is forgiveness of sin.

F 4. According to Evans, repentance originates in man in the same sense that water originates out of a pump.

F 5. Repentance is an example of a responsibility man has the ability to carry out himself.

Note: When Evans says, "Yet this divine gift is brought about by the use of means," this may be confusing. He is explaining that though God's power alone causes repentance to take place, there is a circumstance, or "means," namely the preaching or other communication of the Gospel to the one in need of repentance. The Gospel itself is the "means" by which God brings about repentance.

Paul Preaching at Athens Raphael 1515

Also note that Jonah 3 contains an instance of God "repenting" (not bringing about the disaster foretold) as a result of "repentance" (the people of Nineveh responding to Jonah's preaching by crying to God and turning from evil). This is one of the best illustrations of what repentance truly means when God repents and when man repents. When man is set on a course of action, it results in consequences. If the course is evil, the consequences are judgment. If man repents and changes his evil course to one seeking God's forgiveness and blessing, the consequences are a "repentance," that is, a reversal of the course to judgment and resetting the course to the granting of that forgiveness and blessing. It does not imply that God changed His mind, merely changed the course of His action in accordance with man's response to His warning.

True or False

T 1. Acts 2:37, 38, 41 details the "means" of repentance of 3,000 souls in one day.

F 2. Jonah 3:5-10 makes it clear that before the coming of Christ only Jews could repent and obtain god's forgiveness for sin.

F 3. I Thessalonians 1:5-10 mentions the part that the Holy Ghost plays in repentance three times.

*T*4. Romans 2:4 makes it clear that only God's goodness leads to repentance, and that man has no power to save himself.

T 5. II Peter 3:9 makes it clear that repentance and forgiveness are available to all men.

F 6. Repentance is only necessary for the unsaved, according to Revelation 3:19.

F 7. Chastisement is not a necessary part of the Christian life, according to Hebrews 12:6 ff.

T 8. Repentance is exclusively the work of God. According to II Timothy 2:25 man can only help create the right conditions to bring it about.

F 9. Luke 15:7, 10 describes the part angels play in repentance.

T 10. Isaiah 55:7 is an example of the prophecy described in Acts 3:18-19.

B. Faith

B. Faith

I. THE IMPORTANCE OF THE DOCTRINE.

II. THE DEFINITION OF FAITH.

1. IN GENERAL:

a) Knowledge.

b) Assent.

c) Appropriation.

2. IN PARTICULAR:

a) Towards God.

b) Towards Christ.

c) In Prayer.

d) In the Word of God.

3. RELATION OF FAITH TO WORKS.

III. THE SOURCE OF FAITH.

1. THE DIVINE SIDE.

2. THE HUMAN SIDE.

3. MEANS USED.

IV. SOME RESULTS OF FAITH.

1. SAVED.

2. JOY AND PEACE.

3. DO GREAT WORKS.

Multiple Choice

B 1. All of the following are instances of great faith except

A. Matthew 15:28 B Matthew 16:8 C. Mark 10:52 D. Matthew 8:10

A 2. What Evans describes as Peter's spiritual temple (II Peter 1:5-7) is

A. The spiritual life built on the foundation of faith B. The fruit of the Spirit C. the church built on the Rock mentioned by Christ D. the Beatitudes

B 3. Paul's trinity of grace (I Corinthians 13:13) is

A. Love, Joy, Peace B. Faith, Hope, Love C. Belief, Faith, Trust D. Grace, Hope, Faith

D 4. Psalm 9:10 says that the Lord does not forsake those who

A. obey His Word B. keep His commandments C. copy down His ordinances D. put their trust in Him

A 5. Romans 10:17 states that to have faith people must

A. hear the Word of God B. believe the miracles of Christ C. please God D. memorize the Beatitudes

B 6. Romans 10:14 states that it is impossible to have faith

A. without pleasing God B. without hearing God's Word C. without assembling together D. without a blind leap

C 7. Proverbs 23:7 and Matthew 2:8 both describe

A. the mind of a hypocrite B. the body, soul, and spirit C. complete thought processes D. ceremonial order of worship

D 8. Mark 12:32 demonstrates that the Scribes and Pharisees were

A. ignorant of the Law B. angry with Jesus Christ C. confused about the importance of sacrifices D. capable of understanding what Christ taught

B 9. Matthew 9:28 is one illustration, according to Evans, of faith including all of the following except

A. knowledge of Christ's ability to save B. full knowledge of the Old Testament prophecies C. acknowledgement of Christ's position as Savior of the world D. assenting in the heart that these claims (the heart being man's full spiritual, physical and intellectual being) are true

A 10. John 1:12 states that faith or belief in Christ must be complete in order for a person to

A. Become a son of God B. not be a hypocrite C. fulfill the Law D. observe the Sabbath

D 11. John 2:24 makes it clear that the final determination of a person's acceptance or rejection of Christ lies with

A. the person himself B. the testimony of good men C. the evidence of sincerity D. Christ Himself

D 12. John 20:28 is an example of a verbal testimony Evans says should be followed by

A. performing miracles B. public preaching C. faithful service D. falling down and worshiping

D 13. The Bible describes the people spoken of in John 8:31-59 as

A. Abraham' seed B. Jews who believed on Him (Jesus Christ) C. taking up stones to stone Him D. all of the above

Matching

Write the letter of the verse(s) next to the number of the phrase that best matches the verse's emphasis on the character of God with relation to faith

A. Hebrews 11:6 B. Acts 27:22-25 C. Romans 4:19-21 D. Genesis 15:4-6 E. Luke 11:5-10

A 1. Rewarder of diligence

E 2. Supplier of the Spirit

C 3. Imputer of righteousness

B 4. Protector of life

D 5. Keeper of Promises

Multiple Choice

Write the letter of the "stages" of faith (according to Evans' discussion of faith in the person and work of Christ) next to the Scripture that best matches the concept.

A. Belief in His Person and Deity B. Acknowledgement of His Mission and Work C. Understanding of Christ as coming from God D. Acceptance of Christ as Lord and Savior

B 1. Luke 24:27, 44

D 2. John 8:21, 24

A 3. John 10:30

D 4. Romans 10:9-10

C 5. John 20:28

D 6. John 1:12

A 7. Philippians 2:6-ll

B 8. Matthew 20:28

D 9. John 11:25

B 10. Matthew 26:26-28

A 11. John 9:35-38

C 12. John 16:30

D 13. John 5:24

C 14. Matthew 16:16

C 15. John 6:68, 69

True or False

F 1. I John 5:14, 15 assures us that God grants our petitions before we ask.

T 2. James 1:5-7 encourages us to ask for wisdom.

F 3. Mark 11:24 tells us not to pray for our desires.

T 4. Acts 10:20 relates an unusual answer to prayer.

T 5. Romans 4:20 is an Old Testament instance of faith.

F 6. I Corinthians 10:32 names three groups toward which specific biblical promises might be directed by God: Jews, Gentiles, heretics.

T 7. Titus 1:2 assures us of God's trustworthiness.

Note: Instead of the discussion by Evans on the difference between belief and faith, please read the following excerpt from our book *Antidisestablishmentarianism*. Evans once again resorts to philosophical and confusing language, although the Scriptures from Hebrews 11 and I Kings 18:41-43 are excellent.

And Elijah said unto Ahab, Get thee up, eat and drink; for there is a sound of abundance of rain.

So Ahab went up to eat and to drink. And Elijah went up to the top of Carmel; and he cast himself down upon the earth, and put his face between his knees,

And said to his servant, Go up now, look toward the sea. And he went up, and looked, and said, There is nothing. And he said, Go again seven times.

1 Kings 18:41-43

A true open mind is founded in belief, faith and trust. The historic meaning of believe is to perceive or understand with the mind and then make an informed decision. The most basic use of the word believe which the average American would understand is that of a juror in court. Which witness do you believe? Which piece of evidence is believable? A synonym would be the word credible. When we believe something or someone and then act on that belief, that is faith. The active part of belief is faith. The passive part of belief is trust. Suppose your brother says that he will drive you to the doctor. If you believe him, then you understand what he says and you make a decision to get ready. If you get in the vehicle with him, that is faith. You act on your belief. When you sit in the vehicle as he drives, that is trust, a passive reliance on what you have proven true. You trust in his driving skills. You trust in the vehicle. You trust the roads, etc. Everything we do is a combination of belief, faith or trust.

Matching

Matching

Write A beside the number of the verse if it relates to faith having its source in God or B if the verse relates to the human side of faith.

A 1. Hebrews 12:2

A 2. I Corinthians 12

B 3. Matthew 17: 19-21

A 4. Philippians 1:29

B 5. Luke 11:32

B 6. Luke 17:5, 6

A 7. Matthew 14:30, 31

B 8. Romans 4:19

A 9. Luke 17:5

B 10. Mark 9:24

B 11. Romans 10:17

A 12. Romans 12:3

B 13. Acts 4:4

B 14. Matthew 25:39

A 15. Galatians 5:22

A 16. I Corinthians 12:9

Multiple Choice

Multiple Choice

Choose the letter of the result of faith that best matches the Scripture reference. Write it in the blank next to the number of the verse.

A. Salvation B. Rest, Peace, Assurance, Joy C. Power to serve

B 1. I Peter 1:8

C 2. John 14:12

A 3. John 1:12

A 4. Galatians 3:26

A 5. I Peter 1:5

B 6. Isaiah 26:3

A 7. Romans 5:1

B 8. Romans 5:1

B 9. Hebrews 4:1-3

B 10. John 14:1

C 11. Hebrews 11:32-34

B 12. Philippians 4:6

C 13. Hebrews 11:32-40

C 14. Matthew 21:21

C. Regeneration, or, the New Birth

C. Regeneration, or, the New Birth

I. ITS NATURE.

1. NOT BAPTISM.

2. NOT REFORMATION.

3. A SPIRITUAL QUICKENING.

4. AN IMPARTATION OF A DIVINE NATURE.

5. A NEW AND DIVINE IMPULSE.

II. ITS NECESSITY.

1. UNIVERSAL.

2. THE SINFUL CONDITION OF MAN DEMANDS IT.

3. THE HOLINESS OF GOD DEMANDS IT.

III. THE MEANS.

1. THE DIVINE SIDE.

2. THE HUMAN SIDE.

3. THE MEANS USED.

True or False

T 1. Regeneration is the doorway to Christian discipleship.

F 2. According to Evans, when Jesus speaks of being born of water in John 3:5 he means the water in the womb at birth.

F 3. According to Evans, Titus 3:5 “The washing of Regeneration” is the one verse that could be interpreted to mean that baptism has a part in salvation.

T 4. Ephesians 5:26 says Regeneration comes through the Word of God.

F 5. John 15:3 says that Jesus cleansed the disciples by washing their feet.

F 6. According to James 1:18, the firstfruits symbolized the written Word of God.

T 7. I Peter 1:23 compares seeds to regeneration.

T 8. I Corinthians 4:15 does not mention baptism.

F 9. I Corinthians 1:14 states that Paul did not baptize.

F 10 The baptism of Simon Magus is recorded in Acts 7.

F 11. Cornelius' baptism is recorded in Acts 11.

F 12. Involution means the same as reformation.

F 13. According to Evans, regeneration is a natural, advanced step in human development.

T 14. What Evans means by regeneration being a crisis is that it acknowledges man's natural corruption and need for atonement.

F 15. All of the following passages deal with regeneration: John 3:3-7; John 5:21; Genesis 1:26; Ephesians 2:1, 10; II Corinthians 5:17.

T 16. Ephesians 2:1 and John 5:24 both refer to unregenerate man as being dead.

F 17. In II Peter 1:4, to "be partakers of the divine nature" means receiving eternal life.

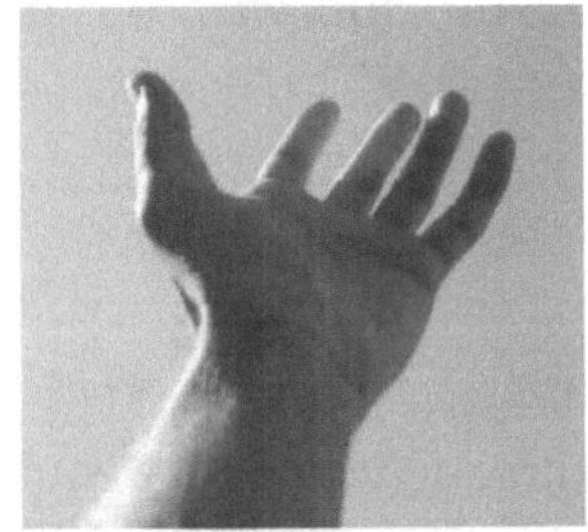

Hand reaching toward Heaven

(Note that Evans lists Ephesians 4:11 under "Regeneration: 4. It is the Impartation of a New Nature -- God's Nature," but Ephesians 4:8 seems to be a better match for this topic. This may be simply a typo.)

T 18. Colossians 3:10 promises a restoration to the image of God we once enjoyed.

F 19. Galatians 2:20 does not deal with spiritual death.

F 20. The I John 3:9 reference to "seed" compares regeneration to the virgin birth.

F 21. Evans explains how Galatians 5:17 contradicts I John 3:9.

T 22. II Corinthians 5:17, Acts 16:14, Ezekiel 36:25-27, and I John 3:6-9 all deal with regeneration making a person able to worship and obey God.

Short Answer

Fill in the blank (or blanks) with the word or phrase that best completes the sentence.

1. According to John 3:3, 5, the only way anyone can see is to be born again. *heaven*

2. Both and are presented as useless to regeneration in Galatians 6:15.
Circumcision and uncircumcision

3. Jeremiah 13:23 compares regeneration to and . *Ethiopians* and *leopards*

4. Romans 8:8 and Romans 7:18 both make the point that the cannot please God. *flesh*

5. Romans 12:2 talks about the contrast between being to this world and by the Spirit. *conformed* and *transformed*

6. Malachi 3:16 speaks of regeneration as believers becoming part of a for "them that feared the Lord, and that thought upon His name."

Book of Remembrance

7. Hebrews 12:14 insists that no man will see the Lord without . *holiness*

8. Ezra 9:15 makes it clear that we cannot stand before God because of . *trespasses*

9. John 1:13 and James 1:18 refer to regeneration as being not by man's but by God's .*will*

10. Evans says that we had no more to do with our second than we had to do with our first . *birth*

11. According to Titus 3:5 and John 3:5, the Holy Spirit is

the Divine of regeneration. *agent*

12. As presented in John 1:12,13, Evans says "The two great problems connected with regeneration are the of God and the of man."

efficiency and activity

(Note that "1 Ep. 1:23" is a misprint for I Peter 1:23)

13. James 1:18, I Corinthians 4:15, and I Peter 1:23 all use the analogy of birth, giving the as the agency of that birth, by the power of the Holy Spirit.

Word of God/truth, Gospel, Scriptures.

14. According to John 1:12, 13 and Galatians 3:26 we become "children of God by in Jesus Christ." *faith*

15. Lazarus' obedience to Christ's command to "Come forth!" from the tomb parallels the part man plays in his salvation. *active*

16. Psalm 90:16,17 and Philippians 2:12,13 explain the two kinds of carried out at the time of salvation: God's first, and then man's response. *work*

D. Justification

D. Justification

I. ITS MEANING.

1. RELATIVELY.

2. SCRIPTURALLY.

3. PARDON--RIGHTEOUSNESS.

II. ITS METHOD.

1. NOT BY LAW.

2. BY GOD'S FREE GRACE.

3. THE BLOOD OF CHRIST.

4. FAITH.

(Note that when Evans says Regeneration is subjective and Justification is objective, he is using these words in the classical, analytical sense. Subjective here means a conclusion drawn from analyzing concrete facts to arrive at an understanding of an abstract concept. Objective means an observable, concrete fact. Regeneration is not, in the modern use of the term, a matter of feeling or opinion. An illustration of this might be: A sign is objective. It is made of metal and paint, and planted beside the road, and contains a message. Identifying the message of the sign, that the bridge ahead is out, as helpful and protective, is subjective.)

Magnifying Glass

Multiple Choice

A 1. In Deuteronomy 25:1, justification is a

A. Judicial term B. Priestly term C. Egyptian term D. Sinatic term

D 2. Romans 4:2-8 includes what Old Testament name(s)?

A. Isaac B. Abraham C. David D. B and C

B 3. Psalm 32:2 is David speaking about

A. need for healing B. need for justification C. need for safety D. need for instruction

C 4. God's delight to pardon is displayed in

A. Psalm 130:4 B. Acts 13:38, 39 C. Micah 7:18, 29 D. Numbers 23:21

D 5. Forgiveness may be considered as

A. as a remission of the punishment of sin, which is eternal death. B. a release from the guilt of sin which oppresses the conscience C. the cessation of the moral anger and resentment of God against sin D. All of the above

C 6. Philemon 18 is a good example of justification because

A. Freeing slaves is like justifying them B. Having a credit account is like justification C. Paying another's debts is like justification D. righting a wrong is like justification

B 7. That justification cannot take place by works of the law is found in all of the following verses except

A. Galatians 3:19, 20 B. II Chronicles 20:8 C. Romans 3:20 D. Galatians 2:16

"2. POSITIVELY: BY GOD'S PEEE GRACE--THE ORIGIN OR SOURCE OF JUSTIFICATION." should read "God's Free Grace."

A 8. Romans 3:24 describes justification that is all of the following except

A. based on merit B. free .C. gracious D. deserved

D 9. "The ground of justification is the of Jesus Christ."

A. life B. example C. work D. blood

B 10. Hebrews 9:22 explains that shedding of blood is essential to

A. communion B. remission C. sacrifice D. translation

True or False

T 1. Evans uses Galatians 2:16 to make the point that faith in Christ is a condition of justification.

T 2. Romans 3:26 points out the source of Jesus Christ's power to justify in His own righteousness.

T 3. Those who live by the works of the law are cursed.

T 4. The best and worst men are saved by faith.

F 5. When Evans says, "works are not meritorious," he means they have no reward.

F 6. Evans' "tree and its fruit" analogy means the same thing as the sower's grain on rocky ground parable.

E. Adoption

E. Adoption

I. THE MEANING OF ADOPTION.

1. ETYMOLOGICALLY.
2. SCRIPTURALLY.

II. THE TIME OF ADOPTION.

1. ETERNAL.
2. WHEN ONE BELIEVES.
3. COMPLETE AT RESURRECTION.

III. THE BLESSINGS OF ADOPTION.

1. FILIAL.
2. EXPERIMENTAL.

IV. SOME EVIDENCES OF SONSHIP.

1. GUIDANCE.
2. CONFIDENCE.
3. ACCESS.
4. LOVE FOR THE BRETHREN.
5. OBEDIENCE.

It is not necessary for the student to master Evans' comparisons between regeneration, justification, and adoption. Carefully reading John 1:12,13 and Galatians 4:1-7 should clarify these distinctions.

True or False

F 1. Galatians 4:1-7 details the process a servant becoming an adult heir.

T 2. Pauline means found in the Pauline Epistles.

F 3. Paul never uses the terms "son" or "child" and John never uses the term adoption.

F 4. Galatians 4:5, Romans 8:15, 23, Romans 9:4, Ephesians 1:5 are examples of Johannine language on adoption.

T 5. Exodus 2:10 and Hebrews 11:24 deal with the same person.

Matching

Matching

Place an A in the blank before the number of Scriptures that support the position that adoption has an eternal aspect, and a B in the blank before the number of Scriptures that support the positions that adoption takes place the moment a person receives Christ and yet is only completed at Christ's coming again.

B 1. II Corinthians 5:10

B 2. I John 3:1-3

A 3. Ephesians 1:4,5

B 4. I John 3:2

A 5 Romans 9:11

B 6 Galatians 3:26

A 7 Romans 11:5,6

B 8 Romans 8:23

B 9 John 1:12

Choose from the following and write the letter of the blessing or evidence of Sonship next to the Scripture it most closely matches (a choice may be used more than once)

A. Object of God's peculiar love B. receivers of God's fatherly care C. bearing the family name D. wearing the family likeness E. experiencing the family love F. enjoying a filial (brotherly) spirit G. having a family service (obedience) H. receiving Fatherly chastisement I. receiving Fatherly comfort J. an inheritance K. led by the Spirit L. childlike confidence in God M. liberty of access (freedom to communicate with God) N. have love for the brethren O. are obedient

I 1. II Corinthians 1:4

E 2. John 13:35

A 3. John 17:23

B 4. Luke 12:27-33

F 5. Romans 8:15

K 6. Galatians 5:18

F 7. Galatians 4:6

G 8. John 14:23,24

C 9. Ephesians 3:14, 15

H 10. Hebrews 12:5-11

I 11. Isaiah 66:13

G 12. John 15:8

N 13. I John 2:9-11

J 14. I Peter 1:3-5

D 15. Romans 8:29

J 16. Romans 8:17

K 17. Romans 8:4

O 18. I John 5:1-3

L 19. Galatians 4:5, 6

M 20. Ephesians 3:12

E 21. I John 3:14

N 22. I John 5:1

C 23. I John 3:1

F. Sanctification

. Sanctification

I. ITS MEANING.

1. NEGATIVELY--SEPARATION FROM EVIL.

2. POSITIVELY--DEDICATION UNTO GOD.

3. USED OF THE DIVINE NATURE.

II. WHEN IT TAKES PLACE.

1. INSTANT.

2. PROGRESSIVE.

3. COMPLETE.

III. THE MEANS.

1. DIVINE.

2. HUMAN.

3. MEANS USED.

Note that some good believers disagree on interpretations of Scriptures related to Sanctification. For the purposes of this study we will not deal with these disagreements but simply follow Evans' interpretations.

Evans's explanation of the progression from Regeneration to Sanctification is fairly easy to follow. The last sentence, dealing with the distinction between justification and sanctification, is especially valuable to consider.

Matching

Write an A in front of the number of the Scriptures that exemplify separation from evil. Write a B in front of the number of the Scriptures that exemplify dedication to God and His service and Sanctification in reference to God Himself.

B 1. Numbers 8:17

A 2. I Thessalonians 4:3

A 3. Hebrews 9:3

B 4. John 10:36

A 5. Exodus 19:20-22

B 6. Ezekiel 36:23

A 7. Leviticus 11:44

A 8. 2 Chronicles. 29:5, 15-18

B 9. Leviticus 27:14,16

Multiple Choice

Write the correct letter of the stage of Sanctification next to the number of the verse it matches

A. Instantaneous B. Progressive C. Final (Complete)

A 1. I Corinthians 6:11

B 2. Ephesians 4:11-15

A 3. I Corinthians 6:11

C 4. I John 3:2

B 5. II Peter 3:18

A 6. I Corinthians 1:2

B 7. II Corinthians 3:18

C 8. I Thessalonians 5:23

B 9. I Thessalonians 3:12

B 10. II Corinthians 7:1

A 11. Hebrews 10:10, 14

B 12. Philippians 3:10-15

A 13. Romans 1:7

C 14. I Thessalonians 3:13

C 15. Philippians 3:12-14

Matching

Matching

Write A next to the number of the verse if it deals with the divine side of sanctification. Write B next to the number of the verse if it deals with the human side.

A 1. Philippians 3:12, 13

A 2. Philippians 2:12, 13

B 3. John 15:3

A 4. John 17:17

A 5. Ephesians 5:25, 27

B 6. John 17:17

A 7. I Corinthians 1:30

B 8. II Corinthians 6:17, 7:1

A 9. I Peter 1:2

A 10. II Thessalonians 2:13

A 11. Galatians 5:17-22

B 12. II Corinthians 1:30

A 13. I Thessalonians 5:23, 24

B 14. Acts 26:18

A 15. Hebrews 12:2

A 16. Philippians 1:6

B 17. Ephesians 5:26

A 18. Hebrews 13:12

B 19. Hebrews 12:14

A 20. Romans 8:2

B 21. Hebrews 12:10, 11

A 22. Hebrews 10:10

B 23. Romans 6:19-32

G. Prayer

I. ITS IMPORTANCE.

II. ITS NATURE.

1. AS SEEN IN ITS HISTORIC DEVELOPMENT.
2. SCRIPTURAL TERMS.

III. ITS POSSIBILITY.

1. THE REVELATION OF GOD.
2. THE WORK OF THE SON.
3. THE ASSISTANCE OF THE SPIRIT.
4. THE PROMISES.
5. CHRISTIAN TESTIMONY.

IV. ITS OBJECTS.

1. GOD THE FATHER.
2. CHRIST THE SON.
3. THE HOLY SPIRIT.

V. ITS METHOD.

1. POSTURE.
2. TIME AND PLACE.

VI. HINDEANCES AND HELPS.

1. HINDRANCES.

2. HELPS--ESSENTIALS.

Fill in the Blank

Complete the sentence with the word or words necessary.

1. Prayer is the Christian's vital . *breath*

2. According to Isaiah 64:7, the neglect of prayer is to the Lord. *grievous*

3. According to Zephaniah 1:4, 6, many in life are to be attributed to the lack of prayer. *evils*

4. (Daniel 9:13) "As it is written in the law of Moses, all this evil is come upon us: yet made we not our before the LORD our God." *prayer*

5. (Hosea 7:14) "And they have not cried unto me with their heart, when they upon their beds." *howled*

6. (I Samuel 12:23) "Moreover as for me, God forbid that I should against the LORD in ceasing to pray for you." *sin*

7. (Col. 4:2) "Continue in prayer, and watch in the same with ." *thanksgiving*

8. (I Corinthians 7:5) According to Evans, we are commanded to take "leisure" or a for prayer. *Vacation*

(Please note that people today think of a vacation as "me time," focusing on doing what is pleasurable to one's self, but imagine the possibilities of a "prayer vacation," taking "time off" focused on communion with the Lord and seeking His will and help.)

9. (Daniel 9:3) "And I set my face unto the Lord God, to seek by prayer and with fasting, and sackcloth, and ashes." *supplications*

10. (Matthew 7:8) "For every one that asketh receiveth; and he that findeth; and to him that knocketh it shall be opened." *seeketh*

11. (James 4:2) This verse teaches that the lack of the necessary blessings in life comes from to pray. *failure*

12. (Romans 1:9) "For God is my witness, ... that without ceasing I make of you always in my prayers." *mention*

13. (Colossians 1:9) "[W]e ... do not cease to pray for you, and to that ye might be with the knowledge of his will in all wisdom and spiritual understanding." *desire, filled*

14. (Genesis 18; 19) "In the life of the patriarch Abraham prayer seems to have taken the form of a . *dialogue*

15. (Genesis 18:31) "And he said, 'Behold now, I have taken upon me to unto the Lord.'" *speak*

16. According to Evans, seems to be the only formal prayer definitely recorded during the period of the giving of the law. *Deuteronomy 26:1-15*

17. (Exodus 32:11) "And Moses the LORD his God, and said, LORD, why doth thy wrath wax hot against thy people,...?" *besought*

18. (1 Samuel 7:5) "And Samuel said, 'Gather all Israel to , and I will pray for you unto the LORD.'" *Mizpeh*

19. (I Samuel 8:18) "And ye shall in that day because of your king which ye shall have chosen you; and the LORD will not hear you in that day." *cry out*

20. (1 Sam. 15:11) "And it Samuel; and he cried unto the LORD all night." *grieved*

21. (II Samuel 7:20) "And what can David say more unto thee? For thou, Lord GOD, knowest thy ." *servant*

22. (I Kings 18:37) "O LORD, hear me, that this people may know that thou art the LORD God, and that thou hast turned their again." *heart back*

23. (Jeremiah 42:4) "Then Jeremiah the prophet said unto them, 'I have you; behold, I will pray unto the LORD your God according to your words' ....." *heard*

24. (Amos 7:2) "And it came to pass, that when they had made an end of eating the grass of the land, then I said, 'O Lord GOD, forgive, I beseech thee: by whom shall arise? for he is small.'" *Jacob*

25. "Consequently the prayers of the psalmist consist of varying : complaint, supplication, confession, despondency, praise. *moods*

26. (Psalm 42:4) "When I remember these things, I pour out my soul in me: ... I went with them to the house of God, with the voice of joy and , with a multitude that kept holyday." *praise*

27. "The closet into which the believer enters to pray is not only an oratory --a place of prayer, it is an , -a place of vision." *observatory*

28. (Isaiah 63:7) "I will mention the of the LORD, and the praises of the LORD, according to all that the LORD hath bestowed on us." *lovingkindnesses*

29. (Hebrews 11:6) "But without faith it is impossible to please him: for he that cometh to God must believe that he is, and that he is a of them that diligently seek him. *rewarder*

30. (Matt. 19:26) Christ reveals God as a God. *sovereign*

31. (Luke 11:13) "If ye then, being evil, know how to give good gifts unto your children: how much more shall your heavenly Father give the to them that ask him?" *Holy Spirit*

32. (Hebrews 10:19-22) "Having therefore, brethren, boldness to enter into the holiest by the blood of Jesus, ... And having an high priest ... Let us draw near with a true heart in full of faith." *assurance*

33. (Romans 8:26) "The Spirit also our infirmities: for we know not what we should pray for as we ought: but the Spirit himself maketh for us with groanings which cannot be uttered." *helpeth, intercession*

Note: Evan says, "The assurance that this verse gives us is that the Holy Spirit will pray within us, and will indict the petition, helping us in our prayer life." The meaning of the word "indict" may be unclear as he uses it here. This is not the meaning "to bring a formal charge against" as we understand it today, but simply to make a formal legal presentation.

34. (Jn 14:13) Whatsoever ye shall ask in my name, that will I do, that the Father may be in the Son. *glorified*

35. (I John 5:14, 15) And this is the that we have...if we ask any thing according to his will, he heareth us: ... whatsoever we ask, we know that we have the that we desired of him. *confidence, petitions*

True or False

F 1. (Nehemiah 4:9) "Nevertheless we made our prayer unto our God, and set a watch against them day and night, because of them," refers to Jewish leaders who undermined Nehemiah's work.

F 2. (II Corinthians 12:8) "For this thing I besought the Lord thrice, that it might depart from me." Paul is referring to the three times he was shipwrecked.

T 3. II Timothy 2:22 lists some of the characteristics of a pure heart.

T 4. Zechariah 12:10 is a prophecy of the giving of the Holy Spirit as well as of the death of Christ.

F 5. Ephesians 6:18 talks about the part of the Christian armor known as the gauntlets of prayer.

F 6. The normal mode of prayer is prayer in the Son, on the ground of the merits of the Spirit, to the Father.

Matching

Matching

Write A in front of the verses that deals with position in prayer. Write B in front of the verse that deal with time of prayer. Write C in front of the verses that deal with the place of prayer.

B 1. Matthew 14:19

A 2. John 17:1

C 3. John 17:1

C 4. Mark 1:35

B 5.John 6:15

A 6. Psalm 63:6

B 7. Exodus 2:23

A 8. Luke 23:42

B 9. Daniel 6:10

B 10. Psalm 55:16, 17

C 11. Acts 16:25

B 12. Acts 3:1

C 13. I Timothy 2:8

B 14. Acts 2:46

A 15. Luke 22:41

B 16. Mark 6:46-48

C 17. Psalm 95:6

B 18. Luke 6:12

B 19. Acts 27:35

B 20. I Timothy 4:4, 5

C 21. Matthew 6:6

A 22. I Kings 8:5

C 24. Matthew 14:23

A 25. Matthew 26:39

C 26. Acts 27:35

B 27. Psalm 81:7

A 28. Matthew 14:30

Matching

Matching

Write A in front of the number of the verse that deals with hindrances to prayer. Write B in front of the number of the verse that deals with helps to prayer.

B 1. Psalm 27:4

B 2. Matthew 6:5

A 3. Isaiah 59:1, 2

B 4. Exodus 14:15

B 5. James 1:6

A 6. Proverbs 28:9

B 7. Matthew 18:19

A 8. James 4:3

B 9. Matt. 21:22

A 10. Matthew 5:22, 23

B 11. Acts 12:5

B 12. Luke 22:44

A 13. Matthew 6:12

B 14. John 16:23

B 15. Colossians 4:2

A 16. Hebrews 11:6

B 17. James 5:17

A 18. James 1:6

A 19. Ezekiel 8:5-18

B 20. Psalm 145:18

A 21. Psalm 66:18

B 22. Matthew 6:7

B 23. Romans 12:12

B 24. Acts 13:2, 3

The Doctrine of the Church

THE DOCTRINE OF THE CHURCH

I. DEFINITION; DISTINCTIONS.

1. OLD TESTAMENT.

2. NEW TESTAMENT.

3. THE CHURCH; CHRISTENDOM; KINGDOM.

II. THE FOUNDING OF THE CHURCH.

1. IN PROPHECY AND PROMISE.

2. HISTORICALLY FOUNDED.

III. MEMBERSHIP IN THE CHURCH.

Conditions of Entrance; Characteristics.

1. REPENTANCE AND BAPTISM.

2. FAITH IN THE DEITY OF JESUS CHRIST.

3. REGENERATION.

4. PUBLIC CONFESSION OF CHRIST--BAPTISM.

5. ADHERENCE TO THE APOSTLES' DOCTRINE.

6. CHARACTERISTICS.

IV. FIGURES UNDER WHICH THE CHURCH IS PRESENTED.

1. THE BODY OF CHRIST.

2. THE TEMPLE OF GOD.

3. THE BRIDE OF CHRIST.

V. THE ORDINANCES OF THE CHURCH.

1. BAPTISM.

2. THE LORD'S SUPPER.

VI. THE VOCATION OF THE CHURCH.

1. TO WORSHIP GOD.

2. TO EVANGELIZE THE WORLD.

3. PERFECT EACH MEMBER.

4. TO WITNESS.

5. FUTURE GLORY.

Church

What Evans means in distinguishing the Church from Christendom is unclear, but is not important for purposes of this study. He does discuss the concepts again under "a) The Church and the Kingdom," below, and there seems to define "Christendom" as those who profess Christ, a group including those who say they are Christians and those who actually possess Christ.

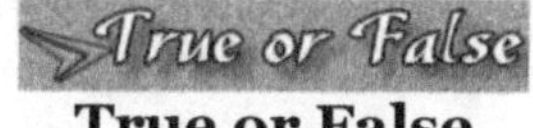

True or False

F 1. In Acts 9 Jesus Christ mentions the church in his speech to Paul.

F 2. Ephesians 5:25 equates the love of Christ for the Church with the love of fathers for their children.

F 3. In I Corinthians 15:9 Paul explains that his persecution of the Church made it stronger.

T 4. Ephesians 4:12 lists three things related to the duties of worthy servants of Christ.

F 5. Evans uses Leviticus 4:13 to teach that the church is a continuation of Israel.

T 6. Acts 7:38 includes a New Testament usage of the Old Testament concept of the congregation of Israel in the wilderness.

F 7. Ecclesia is the Greek word for gathering.

T 8. Ecclesia is used in the New Testament in secular context.

T 9. *Kuriakon* is the Greek word for something belonging to the Lord.

T 10. The apostles headed the first church.

F 11. The second church recorded in the New Testament is at Alexandria.

T 12. The term Church can mean the whole body of Christ, a congregation with a building in a particular location and any meeting of believers.

T 13. There is a church in heaven as well as on earth.

F 14. According to Evans, the distinction between the church militant and the church triumphant is that of a present state and a post-Millennial state.

F 15. The difference between the local church and the universal church is described in I Corinthians 1:2.

Multiple Choice

Multiple Choice

Write the letter of the correct choice in front of the number.

D 1. Christ's prophecy of the church is found in

A. Matthew 18:15-20 B. Matthew 16:16-18 C. John 20:19-23 D. Both A and B

B 2. According to Evans, the "standard of faith" was formed by

A. The Church at Jerusalem B. The Apostles' Doctrine C. The Synagogue D. The Upper Room Meetings

D 3. The church met in

A. believers' homes B. the synagogue C. the temple D. all of the above

C 4. A church roll is

A. a call to prayer B. an order of service C. a count of membership D. a daily meeting

A 5. Proof of regularly organized churches can be found in all the following N.T. books except

A. Matthew B. I Corinthians C. Ephesians D. I Timothy

B 6. All of the following were conditions of church membership except

A. faith in Christ's redemption B. performing signs and wonders C. Salvation/regeneration D. baptism

B 7. All of the following verses teach the need for baptism in the name of the triune God except

A. Acts 10:47 B. Acts 16:30 C. Acts 2:38-39 D. Acts 22:16

A 8. All of the following verses are examples of the teaching of the church as the Body of Christ except

A. Romans 5:12 B. Ephesians 1:22 C. Colossians 2:19 D. Colossians 1:18

C 9. In Romans 12:15-17, all the body parts below are mentioned except

A. eye B. foot C. nose D. hand

B 10. All of the following building terms are used to describe Christ and the church in the New Testament except

A. foundation B. measuring rod C. pillar D. cornerstone

D 11. All of the following marriage terms are used of Christ and the church in the New Testament except

A. Marriage B. Bridegroom C. Bride D. Minister

A 12. When the Lord's Supper is spoken of in the New Testament as being observed on a certain day, that day is

A. the Lord's Day B. the New Moon C. the Passover D. the Sabbath

C 13. Ephesians 1:4-6 teaches us to worship and glorify God on Earth in all the following ways except

A. be holy and without blame B. become His adopted children C. spread His Word to others D. praise and glorify Him for our acceptance in the beloved

D 14. All of the following verses teach evangelizing except

A. Ephesians 3:8 B. Acts 5:42 C. Acts 15:7 D. Acts 6:11

A 15. All of the following gifts are mentioned in Ephesians 4:11-15 except

A. Healers B. Evangelists C. Pastors D. Teachers

A 16. All of the following gifts are mentioned in I Corinthians 12 except

A. gift of helps .....B. the word of wisdom C. the word of knowledge D. faith

C 17. All of the following New Testament verses talk about being a witness for Christ and His Word except

A. Acts 1:8 B. Acts 22:15 C. Matthew 28:18 D. I Peter 5:1

B 18. Revelation 7:9-17 describes the future church as having all of the following except

A. palm branches B. crowns C. white robes D. water

The Doctrine of the Scriptures

THE DOCTRINE OF THE SCRIPTURES.

Bible

I. NAMES AND TITLES.

1. THE BIBLE.

2. THE TESTAMENTS.

3. THE SCRIPTURES.

4. THE WORD OF GOD.

II. INSPIRATION.

1. DEFINITION.

2. DISTINCTIONS.

a) Revelation.

b) Illumination.

c) Reporting.

3. VIEWS:

a) Natural Inspiration.

b) Christian Illumination.

c) Dynamic Theory.

d) Concept Theory.

e) Verbal Inspiration.

f) Partial Inspiration.

g) Plenary Inspiration.

4. THE CLAIMS OF THE SCRIPTURES THEMSELVES:

a) The Old Testament.

b) The New Testament.

5. THE CHARACTER (OR DEGREES) OF INSPIRATION.

a) Actual Words of God Himself.

b) Actual Words Communicated by God to Men.

e) Individual Freedom in Choice of Words--To What Extent?

Short Answer

Fill in the blank(s) with the word or words that best complete the statement.

1. The word *biblos* means book and comes from one of the names of the material books were written on, . *papyrus*

2. "The Bible is ...the Book that from ... the of its Author, stands as high above all other books as the heaven is high above the earth. *majesty*

3. "The word Testament means , and is the term by which God was pleased to designate the relation that existed between Himself and His people." *covenant*

4. ", in the beginning of the third century, mentioned 'the divine Scriptures, the so-called Old and New Covenants.'" *Origen*

5. The OT is history of the Jews. The NT is of redemption by Jesus Christ. *application*

6. The “Scriptures” was the most common designation for the whole Bible by the early . *Christians*

7. The name given for the Bible that is “the most significant, impressive, and complete” is .*the Word of God*

8. According to Evans, II Timothy 3:16 deals with the Testament. *Old*

9. According to Evans, three examples of Greek words he gives referring to breath mean to breathe gently, to breathe forcibly, and to breathe . *unconsciously*

10. “The Scriptures are the result of divine , just as human speech is uttered by the breathing through a man’s mouth.” *inbreathing*

11. “... Holy men of God wrote the Scripture when to do so by the Holy Spirit.” *moved*

12. “... The Holy Ghost was especially and miraculously present with and in writers of the Scriptures, to them truths they did not know before ...” *revealing*

13. “And guiding them in their record of these truths, and of the of which they were eye and ear witnesses, they were enabled to present with accuracy to t others. *transactions, substantial*

14. “The Bible is indeed and in the very Word of God, and the books of the Bible are of divine and authority.” *truth, origin*

True or False

T 1. Revelation is truth which a writer could have learned in no other manner.”

T 2. Inspiration demands that the history recorded in the Bible be true.

F 3. The book of Job gives equal authority to the words of God, Satan, Job and his three friends.

F 4. The record of Creation is an example of Verbatim Reporting.

F 5. Moses' account of the Exodus is an example of Revelation.

T 6. Inspiration superintends the communicating of truth in the Scriptures.

T 7. Paul's account of his interview with Peter at Antioch is an example of God using the writer's memory, personality and judgment as part of the inspired account.

F 8. Things not sanctioned by God, recorded in the Bible, are not to be considered inspired.

T 9. The words of Satan, Job, and his three friends were not originally spoke by inspiration of God.

F 10. Evans says David's cruelty to the Ammonites is recorded in the book of Kings with God's evident disapproval, just as the incidents of murder and adultery.

T 11. Man cannot understand a statement of a truth about God or spiritual things unless the Holy Spirit reveals it to him.

F 12. "The Scriptures are not in any way the oracles of God, nor do they come to us as direct, logical utterances of the divine mind."

T 13. Evans presents the Illumination Theory as teaching that the Bible records the words of holy men attuned to the mind of God who wrote down their understanding of Him to us.

F 14. We have no examples in the Bible where God revealed Himself, His truth, and His will to men who were not engaged in meditating upon Him.

F 15. The prophecy of Caiaphas concerning Jesus' death was an example in support of the Illumination Theory.

F 16. Numbers 22:34-35 is an example of how God provided illumination through Moses.

T 17. Verbatim Recording implies that the writers performed a mechanical operation.

T 18. Natural Inspiration identifies inspiration with genius of a high order.

F 19. Isaiah said, "The Spirit of the Lord spake by me, and His word was in my tongue," to establish the inspiration of his words.

F 20. "Which things also we speak, not in the words which man's wisdom teacheth, but which the Holy Ghost teacheth," is spoken by Peter.

T 21. Mechanical, or dynamic, Inspiration teaches that the Holy Spirit animated the writers to create Scriptures without their conscious participation.

F 22. "The Bible contains the Word of God" sums up the theory Concept or Though Inspiration.

T 23. "Partial Inspiration ... leaves man in awful and fatal uncertainty."

T 24. The Revised Version translation of 2 Tim. 3:16 is erroneous because it implies that some Scripture is not inspired.

F 25. The spirit of rationalism supports Divine inspiration.

T 26. The identical Greek construction for the use of the word translated "also" in II Timothy 3:16 is rendered differently in Hebrews 4:13 in the RV translation.

F 27. No writers of Scriptures claimed divine inspiration for their words.

T 28. Exodus 4:10-15 makes the point that Moses resisted being used by God to communicate His Word, and therefore had no personal "Illumination" to write the Scriptures.

T 29. Deuteronomy 4:2 makes the point that God Himself gave the commandments He wanted kept, no more and no less.

T 30. God comforted the fears of His prophets with the promise that He would put His words in their mouths."

T 31. Scriptures indicating God's direct speech or words number in excess of 3000 times in the Old Testament alone.

F 32. New Testament writers did not claim inspiration for Old Testament writers.

Matching

Matching

Write the letter A in front of the number of the verse if it is an example of recording the exact Words of God. Write a B if it is an example of God "putting into the mouth" words to be said or written down. Write C if the verse is an example of writers choosing their own words to communicate divine truth. Write D if speakers spoke without knowing or understanding what their words meant.

A 1. Exodus 38:16

A 2. Deuteronomy 9:10

B 3. Habakkuk 2:2

D 4. Mark 1:11

A 5. Exodus 24:12

B 6. Isaiah 8:1, 11, 12

D 7. Luke 3:22

A 8. Matthew 3:17

B 9. Exodus 4:10-15

A 10. Exodus 31:18

B 11. I Corinthians 14:37

B 12. Revelation 10:4

C 13. John 11:49-52

A 14. Deuteronomy 10:2, 4

C 15. Daniel 12:8, 9

A 16. I Chronicles 28:19

D 17. Luke 1:1-4

B 18. Jeremiah 30:1, 3

D 19. Matthew 26:26, 27

A 20. Daniel 5:5

B 21. Jeremiah 13:12

D 22. Luke 22:19, 20

B 23. Exodus 34:27

D 24. I Corinthians 11:24, 25

B 25. Jeremiah 1:7

B 26. Zechariah 7:8-12

D 27. Matthew 3:17

B 28. Numbers 17:2, 3

B 29. Ezekiel 2:7

C 30. Numbers 22:28-30

B 31. Ezekiel 3:10, 11

The Doctrine of Angels

THE DOCTRINE OF ANGELS.

Angel

I. THEIR EXISTENCE.

1. THE TEACHING OF JESUS.
2. THE TEACHING OF THE APOSTLES.

II. THEIR NATURE.

1. CREATED BEINGS.
2. SPIRITUAL BEINGS.
3. GREAT POWER AND MIGHT.
4. VARIOUS GRADES.
5. THE NUMBER OF ANGELS.

III. THE FALL OF ANGELS.

1. TIME AND CAUSE.
2. THE WORK OF FALLEN ANGELS.
3. THE JUDGMENT OF FALLEN ANGELS.

IV. THE WORK OF ANGELS.

1. THEIR HEAVENLY MINISTRY.

2. THEIR EARTHLY MINISTRY.

a) In Relation to the Believer.

b) In Relation to Christ's Second Coming.

Evans' introduction to this topic makes the very important point that rationalists and materialists will take any occasion they can to chip away at spiritual belief. Angels are a subject in the Bible about which many things are mysterious, and there is a temptation to ignore or disbelieve in the doctrine because it is purely a spiritual matter, not a daily living matter. It may seem "less important," or might have little to do with evangelism or even edification. But angels are part of the "whole counsel of God," and giving all the Scriptures their proper authority means giving angels a place in the realm of reality.

True or False

F 1. All of the references Evans gives where Jesus Christ mentions angels refer to them as doing battle or coming in judgment.

T 2. In II Thessalonians 1:7 those suffering persecution are promised rest when Christ returns with His angels.

T 3. Colossians 2:18 states that worshiping angels is a heresy.

T 4. John 1:51 presents an image similar to that in Genesis 28:12.

F 5. Revelation 12:7 tells the incident where Michael the archangel disputes Satan for the body of Moses.

F 6. The angel John attempted to worship in Revelation 22:8-9 was Gabriel.

F 7. The subject of I Peter 3:22 ("Who is gone up to heaven") is Satan.

T 8. II Peter 2:10-12 confirms that angels are greater in power and might than men.

F 9. Jude verse 9 records the casting out of Satan from heaven by Michael.

T 10. Luke 22:43 records the second occasion when angels specifically strengthened or ministered to Christ in His earthly life.

T 11. In Hebrews 12:18-22, Mount Sinai is contrasted with Mount Zion because the former is a place of fear and the latter is a place of welcome.

T 12. Hebrews 12:22,23 indicates that angels are created beings, distinct from humans.

T 13. Hebrews 1:14 implies that angels serve those who are redeemed.

T 14. Many Scriptures dealing with miraculous events refer to one angel and many also refer to thousands of angels.

F 15. The Bible mentions seven angels by name.

T 16. Angels that sinned are spoken of in Jude 6 as being chained.

F 17. The time of the fall of the angels is recorded as occurring between Genesis 1:1 and 1:2.

F 18. Deuteronomy 32:8 describes the "first estate" or proper divisions of the angels.

T 19. The Prince of the Kingdom of Persia in Daniel 10:13 is recorded as withstanding an angel.

F 20. I Corinthians 6:3 indicates that God alone will judge the fallen angels.

Matching

Write the letter of the earthly ministry of angels that best matches the verse next to the number of that verse.

A. Bless the Lord with their strength and obedience B. Captain of the Lord's Host C. Spirits ministering in flame D. Elijah fed while fleeing Jezebel E. Peter released from prison F. Showed Hagar the well in the wilderness G. Bringing plague as judgment H. Stand up for Israel I. Ministering to heirs of salvation J. Promised Paul safety in Shipwreck K. Philip sent to Ethiopian Eunuch L. Cornelius told to send for Peter M. minister to Christ after temptation N. minister to Christ in Gethsemane O. Daniel delivered from lions P. Elisha defended against Syrians Q. Men of Sodom blinded R. Witnessing charges to church elders S. Observing conduct of apostles T. Involved in women's modesty U. Carry saved to heaven V. Taking vengeance on disobedient

T 1. I Corinthians 11:10

O 2. Daniel 6:22

F 3. Genesis 21:17

K 4. Acts 8:26

U 5. Luke 16:22

R 6. I Timothy 5:21

B 7. Joshua 5:15

P 8. II Kings 6:17

S 9. I Corinthians 4:9

L 10. Acts 10:3

M 11. Matthew 4:11

Q 12. Genesis 19:11

E 13. Acts 12:7

N 14. Luke 22:43

D 15. I Kings 19:5

V 16. II Thessalonians 1:8

I 17. Hebrews 1:14

J 18. Acts 27:24

Satan and his Dragon alter ego.

THE DOCTRINE OF SATAN.

I. HIS EXISTENCE AND PERSONALITY.

1. EXISTENCE.

2. PERSONALITY.

II. HIS PLACE AND POWER.

1. A MIGHTY ANGEL.

2. PRINCE OF POWER OF THE AIR.

3. GOD OF THIS WORLD.

4. HEAD OF KINGDOM OF DARKNESS.

5. SOVEREIGN OVER DEATH.

III. HIS CHARACTER.

1. ADVERSARY.

2. DIABOLOS.

3. WICKED ONE.

4. TEMPTER.

IV. OUR ATTITUDE TOWARDS SATAN.

1. LIMITED POWER OF SATAN.

2. RESIST HIM.

V. HIS DESTINY.

1. A CONQUERED ENEMY.

2. UNDER ETERNAL CURSE.

VI. DEMONS.

Evans' point that we should study the Scriptures and "know thine enemy" is well-taken. However, godly men like Milton and Luther, though their works are not inspired Scripture, have experienced Satan's power to damage and hinder God's servants. Their writings about Satan were certainly not intended as mockery. Sinners will mock God's Word and His people and mock their attempts at teaching and warning other believers to make a mockery at any opportunity. He is correct that many try to claim Satan is not a person and that this false view needs to be challenged.

Evans also seems to be falling into the trap of divorcing Science from belief as so many have been led to do. He claims that science can neither confirm nor deny the existence of Satan. Belief is testing the evidence. Faith is acting on what belief has proved, and the evidence of Scripture about the existence of Satan is as scientific as could be wished.

Short Answer

1. Matthew 13:19, 38 both use as an analogy of man and his reception of God's Word. *grain, crops, farming, sowing, fields all possible answers*

2. John 13:2 is an example of Satan's ability to sin to our minds. *suggest*

3. The sin Satan tempted Ananias and Sapphira to was lying to . *the Holy Spirit*

4. II Corinthians 11:3 says being corrupted from the simplicity that is in Christ was like the serpent Eve. *beguiling*

5. According to II Corinthians 11:3 Satan can be transformed into . *an angel of light*

6. II Peter 2:1-4 compares to angels who sinned in terms of the certainty of God's punishment for sin. *false prophets*

7. Ezekiel 28:16 and Isaiah 14:12-14 both imply that Satan was cast out because of his desire to .
rule, have control, be supreme are all possible answers

(Note that there appears to be an error in referencing John 8:44 as proving that Satan was once "in the truth." A verse that may support that position is Ezekiel 28:15, if, as Evans notes, this passage refers to Satan.)

8. John 8:44 designates Satan as the of lying. *father*

9. Luke 10:18: "And he said unto them, I beheld Satan as fall from heaven." *lightning*

10. I Timothy 3:6 "Not a , lest being lifted up with pride he fall into the condemnation of the devil." *novice*

11. Matthew 25:41 indicates that the "everlasting fire" was created for the devil and . *his angels*

12. I John 3:8: "He that committeth sin is of the devil; for the devil sinneth from ." *the beginning*

13. Hebrews 2:14 says that Satan has power over . *death*

14. In John 14:30 Jesus calls Satan the " of this world." *prince*

15. Zechariah 3:1 shows Satan as God's people. *resisting*

16. I Chronicles 21:1 shows that Satan has the ability to God's people to sin. *provoke*

17. Ephesians 2:2 describes Satan as the spirit working in the of disobedience. *children*

18. In Matthew 12:24 Satan was called, "Beelzebub, of demons." *prince*

19. II Corinthians 4:4 describes the influence of Satan as the mind. *blinding*

20. "Satan is not only the object of the world's worship, but also the spirit of its godless activities." *moving*

21. Acts 26:18 and Colossians 1:13 contrast kingdom of God and kingdom of Satan as light and . *darkness*

22. I Peter 5:8 refers to the Devil primarily as an . *adversary*

23. In Numbers 22:22, the angel that stood in Balaam's way is an example of an . *adversary*

24. Revelation 12:9 depicts Satan as the whole world. *deceiving*

25. Genesis 3 and Job 1 are examples of Satan's ability to . *slander*

26. I John 5:19 contrasts our security in God with the world, which "lieth in . *wickedness*

27. Matthew 4:1-11 is an example of Satan trying to deceive by suggesting the use of in a wrong way. *right things*

28. (II Thessalonians 2:9) "Even him, whose coming is after the working of Satan with all power and signs and ." *lying wonder*

29. (John 12:31) "Now is the of this world: now shall the prince of this world be cast out. *judgment*

30. (Matthew 8:31) "So the devils , saying, 'If thou cast us out, suffer us to go away into the herd of swine.'" *besought him*

31. (James 4:7) "Resist the devil, and he from you." *will flee*

32. Isaiah 65:25 proclaims the end of the curse on the earth, yet the serpent is portrayed as eating . *dust*

33. Revelation 20:10 acknowledges that Satan will be a to the end. *deceiver*

The Doctrine of Last Things

THE DOCTRINE OF THE LAST THINGS.

A. THE SECOND COMING OF CHRIST.

B. THE RESURRECTION.

C. THE JUDGMENT.

D. THE DESTINY OF THE WICKED.

E. THE REWARD OF THE RIGHTEOUS.

A. THE SECOND COMING OF CHEIST.

I. ITS IMPORTANCE.

1. PROMINENCE IN THE SCRIPTURES.

2. THE CHRISTIAN HOPE.

3. THE CHRISTIAN INCENTIVE.

4. THE CHRISTIAN COMFORT.

II. ITS NATURE.

1. PERSONAL AND VISIBLE COMING TO THE EARTH.

2. DIFFERENT VIEWS.

3. DISTINCTIONS.

III. ITS PURPOSE.

WITH REFERENCE TO--

1. THE CHURCH.

2. THE UNREGENERATE.

3. THE JEWS.

4. THE ENEMIES OF GOD.

5. THE MILLENNIUM.

IV. ITS DATE.

1. DAY AND HOUR UNKNOWN.

2. RECOGNIZING THE “SIGNS.”

3. IMMINENT.

True or False

T 1. I Peter 1:11 refers to Old Testament writers.

F 2. John 21:22 states that John would remain alive until Christ returned.

T 3. Hebrews 2:2 makes the point that the testimony of angels is trustworthy.

F 4. The "times of refreshing" spoken of in Acts 3:19 refer to the giving of the Holy Spirit.

T 5. The point of Hebrews 9:28 is that Christ's death was an atonement resulting in His being able to return for believers without any sin of theirs to deal with.

T 6. I John 2:28 tells how to have confidence when Christ appears.

T 7. Jude 14 recounts what may be the earliest prophecy of the end times.

(Note that we have no prophecy by Enoch in the Scriptures we have, and we do not know the source of Jude's record, though we believe this passage is part of God's inspired Word. The book known as the Book of Enoch, included as part of the Apocrypha in some Bibles, is not considered inspired and is not the source for this.)

F 8. II Peter 3:12, 13 expresses Peter' eagerness to see the world destroyed.

F 9. Matt. 24:44-46 and Luke 21:34-36 state that we can live however we want because Christ's second coming will wipe out any sin we have committed.

T 10. I John 3:3 teaches that the hope of the Second Coming is an incentive to live a pure life.

F 11. II Peter 3:4 corrects his earlier mistaken statements about the Lord's return.

T 12. I Corinthians 15:51 says that not everyone will die.

F 13. Philippians 3:20 teaches that we should talk about heaven to make the Lord return sooner.

F 14. No prophecies about the Second Coming occur after the giving of the Holy Spirit.

F 15. The Second Coming is a single event, one point of time.

Matching

Matching

Write the letter of the correct aspect of the purpose of the Second Coming in front of the number of the verse it refers to.

A. Believers to meet Christ in the air B. Marriage of the Church (bride) to the Lord C. Believers' rewards D. Judgments on the Nations and others E. regarding the Jews F. Regarding the Antichrist and other enemies G. Millennium

D 1. Matthew 25:31, 32

B 2. Revelation 19:6-9

D 3. Revelation 20:11, 12

A 4. I Corinthians 15:50-52

C 5. II Corinthians 5:10

A 6. I John 3:2

E 7. Daniel 9:27

E 8. Zechariah 12:10

B 9. Ephesians 5:23, 32

B 10. II Corinthians 11:2

A 11. Philippians 3:20, 21

B 12. Matthew 25:1-10

C 13. II Timothy 4:8

E 14. Ezekiel 34:28

C 15. I Corinthians 3:12-15

D 16. Matthew 24:30

A 17. I Thessalonians 4:13-17

D 18. II Thessalonians 1:7-9

E 19. Matthew 24:21, 22, 29

C 20. Matthew 25:19

E 21. Isaiah 11:11; 60

C 22. I Peter 5:4

E 23. II Thessalonians 2

G 24. Revelation 19:11-14

E 25. Revelation 3:10; 7:14

E 26. Zechariah 8:13-23

F 27. II Thessalonians 1:7-9

G 28. Revelation 19:20

E 29. Revelation 1:7

F 30. Revelation 20:10

G 31. Revelation 20:1-4

G 32. Daniel 7:21, 22

D 33. Revelation 1:7

F 34. Revelation 19:20

E 35. Amos 9:15

D 36. Isaiah 26:21

G 37. Matthew 24:29,30

E 38. Ezekiel 40-48

G 39. Zechariah 14:3-9

G 40. Jeremiah 23:5

Multiple Choice

Multiple Choice

Write the letter of the word or phrase in front of the number of the statement that it completes.

B 1. The word "Parousia" means

A. Saints B. Rapture C. Epiphany D. signs

C 2. According to Luke 21:29-33, the Second Coming should not A. affect anyone but believers B. happen suddenly C. catch us by surprise D. result in any unsaved being converted

D 3. I Timothy 4:1 says that some will the faith.

A. lie about B. come back to C. completely destroy D. depart from

D 4. James 5:1-9 condemns

A. hoarding wealth B. cheating workers C. condemning the just D. all of the above

A 5. Matthew 24:14 states that before the Second Coming the gospel will be preached

A. in all the world B. throughout Judea C. to all Jews D. in unknown lands

flag of Israel

Note: Concerning Evans' statements about Israel, by way of reminder, this book was published in 1912. The physical founding of the Jewish State of Israel (independence declared in 1947, armistice in 1949) had not yet happened. It was thought by many to be the certain sign of Christ's return. Just a reminder that the Bible talks about many different signs of the Second Coming, and focusing on one or another as more important can lead to mistaken conclusions.

B 6. Evans states that nothing hinders the Rapture, but that the is a separate event.

A. preaching to all the world B. coming with the saints C. passing of "this generation" D. destruction of Jerusalem

D 7. "This generation" (Matthew 24:34 and other passages), according to Evans, can refer to all of the following except

A. destruction of Jerusalem B. Jewish Race C. forty years D. the lifetime of John

B. THE RESURRECTION OF THE DEAD.

I. THIS DOCTRINE CLEARLY TAUGHT IN THE SCRIPTURES.

1. IN THE OLD TESTAMENT.

2. IN THE NEW TESTAMENT.

II. THE NATURE OF THE RESURRECTION.

1. LITERAL RESURRECTION OF THE BODIES OF ALL MEN.

2. RESURRECTION OF THE BODY NECESSARY TO COMPLETE SALVATION.

3. THE NATURE OF THE RESURRECTION BODY.

a) In General.

b) The Body of the Believer.

c) The Body of the Unbeliever.

III. THE TIME OF THE RESURRECTION.

1. OF THE RIGHTEOUS.

2. OF THE WICKED.

Fill-in-the-Blank

Fill in the Blank

1. Job 19:25-27 teaches a resurrection. *bodily*

2. Hebrews 11:17-19 says that the preservation of Isaac was resurrection "in a ." *figure*

3. II Kings 13:21 records the resurrection by contact with the bones of . *Elisha*

4. According to Evans, Mark 9:10 indicates that the disciples did not the teaching about Christ's crucifixion. *accept*

5. In John 6:39, "all that the Father hath given me" refers to Jesus' *disciples*

6. Acts 24:15 refers to a dispute among sects of Judaism concerning the . *resurrection of the dead.*

7. The events of Matthew 27:52-53 indicate that even before Christ's resurrection there were true . *believers (saints)*

8. Psalm 16:9 indicates that the believer's hope of resurrection includes as well as spirit. *body*

Note: Evans tries to deal with "literaliz(ing) these Scriptures which are intended to be metaphorical and spiritual." He is attempting to combat those who rob Scriptures of literal meaning. This quote is hard to understand. "Indeed John 5:25-29 draws a sharp contrast between a spiritual (v. 25) and a literal (v. 28) resurrection." It refers to a literal resurrection. The only "spiritual" component of the verses might be that the verses mention damnation and allude to salvation, which are spiritual elements of the resurrection. Ephesians 5:14 refers to an awakening of spiritual understanding and has nothing to do with the resurrection. Perhaps this is what Evans means by spiritual resurrection. This discussion is unclear and can be ignored.

9. Romans 8:13 refers to both the and the of the body in the resurrection. *adoption, redemption*

10. Philippians 3:21 speaks of God changing our bodies to be like His body. *vile, glorious*

11. II Corinthians 5:4 says that Paul doesn't desire to be rid of his body, or his "clothing," but that his " might be swallowed up in ." *mortality, life*

12. I Corinthians 15:35ff explain that our resurrection body is comparable to the difference between a and the plant that grows from it. *seed*

13. I John 3:2 states that we may not fully understand our resurrection bodies but we know that they will be like . *Christ's*

14. (I Corinthians 15:23)"But every man in his own order: Christ the ; afterwards they that are Christ's at his coming." *firstfruits*

15. (Daniel 12:2) "And many of them that sleep in the dust of the earth shall awake, some to everlasting life, and some to and everlasting . *shame, contempt*

16. At least years passes between the resurrections of the righteous and the wicked. *1000*

17. Evans suggests that if there is something difficult or hard to understand about the resurrection, we should remember Jesus Christ's statement in (reference) , "Ye do err, not knowing the scriptures, nor the power of God." *Matthew 22:29*

C. THE JUDGMENT.

I. THE FACT OF THE JUDGMENT.

1. AS TAUGHT IN THE OLD TESTAMENT.

2. AS TAUGHT IN THE NEW TESTAMENT.

3. THE TESTIMONY OF CONSCIENCE.

4. THE TESTIMONY OF CHRIST'S RESURRECTION.

II. THE JUDGE--CHRIST.

III. THE NATURE OF THE JUDGMENT.

1. JUDGMENT AT THE CROSS.

2. THE DAILY JUDGMENT.

3. FUTURE JUDGMENT.

a) Of the Saints.

b) Of the Living Nations.

c) Of the Great White Throne.

d) Of the Fallen Angels.

e) Of Israel.

True or False

T 1. According to Evans, the "judging" in Psalm 96:13 includes both rewards and punishments.

T 2. Paul, in I Corinthians 15:19, says that Christians are to be pitied if their only hope in Christ is in this life.

F 3. According to Evans, John 11:11 supports the belief in "soul sleep."

F 4. The parable of the Talents pictures caring for the inward spiritual life and the parable of the ten virgins pictures caring for the outward life in service to God.

T 5. The parable of the Talents deals with gifts compatible with a person's ability.

T 6. The Scriptures speak in different places of various specific types of crowns and in others of one crown.

F 7. The Tree of Life is not mentioned between Genesis and Revelation.

F 8. The "Second Death" refers only to Satan and the Beast and False Prophet.

F 9. The White Stone refers to the material from which the Great White Throne of Judgment was made.

T 10. Evans says the "Hidden Manna" may mean a reward for resisting eating meat offered to idols.

T 11. Being given a new name may refer to having a new identity as a "sanctified citizen."

F 12. The concept of the Book of Life is only mentioned in the New Testament.

F 13. The church at Philadelphia had "pillars" (important members) who failed to support the church, leading to the analogy of making believers pillars in the New Temple.

F 14. Revelation makes it clear that no one will sit on Christ's right and left hands, as John and James desired.

T 15. The New Jerusalem will be more than 100 times the size of the old earthly one.

T 16. The New Jerusalem will include new creations.

Research/Thought/Essay Questions

Research/Thought/Essay

Please note that in recommending partial answers or tools for research we have not studied these subjects or sources exhaustively and are only trying to suggest aids which might be helpful. Sometimes outsiders present a religion inaccurately, sometimes insiders do as well. Have students study several sources and try to arrive at a general picture of what the "believers believe." As far as research sources go, this is up to the teacher, but we do most of our research online. Wikipedia is actually a good starting point to gather sources, but it should not be "the" source. Many respected older research works are now available online, extensive excerpts from books and articles, and websites devoted to Biblical authority and hundreds of other topics. The teacher can adapt, limit, simplify or modify these projects as needed. They need not be lengthy written works. Visual projects, dioramas, posters, assembling pictures and text in a PowerPoint or simple video presentation are also good ideas. Even craft projects can be used to complete the requirements.

1. Many religions, including some claiming to be based on the Bible, claim that God exists but is a) not a person (a creative force, part of nature or existing as part of a whole collective life force including man, animals and everything) or b) was Creator but is no longer involved or not personally interested in His creation or man. Refute some of these positions with verses Evans brings out. The student may wish to choose a specific religion, like Deism, Buddhism, Pantheism (which is taught within a number of specific religions), Arianism or Socinianism to refute.

Many of the founding fathers of America professed to be Deists, so an examination of their lives could be done. Thomas Paine claimed to be a Deist but most of his contemporaries repudiated him after the publication of the Age of Reason, a bitter attack on Christianity. Ellen Judy Wilson and Peter Hanns Reill, Encyclopedia of the Enlightenment (2004) discusses deism in 80 different articles on leading intellectuals.
http://www.deism.com/ is a resource by deists about Deism.

www.sacredtexts.com includes texts of Buddhism. www.religioustolerance.org and www.pbs.org/edens/thailand/buddhism.htm have basic explanations of the belief system. www.plato.stanford.edu/entries/pantheism/ has a discussion on Pantheism.

2. Several passages in the Scriptures are parodies and satires on the subject of idol worship. Isaiah 44:6-20 and Jeremiah 10: 1-15 are examples. Using these as a basis, have the student write a modern satire or parody of man's worship of things like money, possessions, self, or celebrities. There are even modern examples of "idol" worship such as in India where young girls or deformed babies are called gods.

One of the most famous satires of all times on the subject of how materialism leads to indifference and depravity is "A Modest Proposal" by Jonathan Swift in 1729. In response to British scorn or apathy toward Irish poverty Swift wrote the piece suggesting that the Irish might sell their children as food to the wealthy.

3. Have the student make a refutation of the teachings of such false beliefs as Unitarianism and Monotheism that excludes the possibility of the Trinity. Note that the beliefs of Unitarianism are by no means "unified" and a student will have to pick and choose what to bring out about their teachings. Islam is a good example of a monotheistic religion but has many sects and is also difficult to pin down. Judaism might be easier to study but the students should use other sources besides just the Scriptures.

Unitarians believe to varying degrees that Jesus Christ was either just a good teacher, possibly indwelt by the Holy Spirit, or that there was a separate preexisting spirit, the Logos, who indwelt Jesus Christ at some point or points in His earthly life, or that Jesus was a created being superior to men but inferior to and separate from God Himself. They believe He was a good example, a pattern for life, and that He did not claim to be God or equal to God. http://www.uua.org/beliefs/history/6903.shtml is the official website of the Unitarian Universalist church. Islam resources include www.religioustolerance.org World Religions or www.islam101.com/ . Sites for studying Judaism include www.jewfaq.org/

4. John Tyndall, quoted by Evans as saying, "I have noticed that it is not during the hours of my clearness and vigor that the doctrine of material atheism commends itself to my mind," was a physicist in the mid-1800's who actually supported evolution and Darwinism. Try to explain this quote in the context of Tyndall's work and beliefs. Note also that Tyndall's support of Darwinism was not the position of the majority of scientists in his day.

Tyndall was a personal friend of Thomas Henry Huxley, who was known as "Darwin's Bulldog." A speech in 1874 which he gave as president of the British Association for the Advancement of Science in 1874 spoke favorably of Evolution and Darwin, repeatedly using his name. He finished by saying that belief must not "intrude on the region of knowledge, over which it holds no command."

5. Robert Browning and Charles Lamb both professed faith in Jesus Christ. Research the lives of one or both of these writers and in a short project explain how their faith influenced their work.

Robert Browning was a Romantic poet who satirized the Roman Catholic church's hypocrisy but respected and praised true faith in God. A good poem to study is "Rabbi Ben Ezra." Charles Lamb and his wife Mary sought to educate young readers about the truth of God as expressed in the classic virtues of great literature. Both writers combated the dark and anti-God tone of other poets.

6. Research the Gnostic heresy, including the theory of emanations. Who fought against it historically, why is it

dangerous, and what are the arguments of Scriptures against it?

Gnosticism is extremely varied and complicated in its beliefs. The existence of many spirits which "emanated" from a distant and uninvolved god or two gods equal in power but opposing one another are key beliefs. These "lesser" spirits are imperfect, sometimes ignorant, sometimes evil. Asceticism or extreme denial of the physical self is another common belief. Several sources mention the "Nag Hammadi Library" as a collection of Gnostic books. http://findleyfamilyvideopublications.com/exhibit2gallery3artifact3.html is a link to our website, in the Virtual Museum Exhibit of ancient manuscripts related to the Bible. It has a brief article about these books which may be helpful. Eusebius and Athanasius, among others, preached against Gnosticism.

7. Research the "accident theory" of Christ's death. Who subscribes to this belief and why? Look up the Scriptures that refute it and comment briefly on some of them.

(There are many more than Evans' list included here, but these are good ones.) Matt. 16-21 Mark 9:30-32 Matt. 20:17-19 Luke 18:31-34 Matt. 20:28 Matt. 26:2, 6, 24, 39-42 Luke 22:19, 20 John 10:17, 18 Luke 24:26, 27, 44 Isa. 53 Psa. 22 Psa. 69.

8. Isaiah Chapters 11 and 35 are used by Evans to support the point VI. THE EFFECTS OF CHRIST'S DEATH. 1. IN RELATION TO THE PHYSICAL OR MATERIAL UNIVERSE. Have the student 1. Create a picture or poster in whatever media desired or 2. Write a descriptive essay or 3. Compose a poem including details from these passages that support the point that the Creation will be very different from what we see now.

This assignment will produce widely varying results. The teacher should basically look for clarity in the inclusion and presentation of some of the major points in the Isaiah chapters specified. It is not an open-ended or purely "creative" assignment because the student must include identifiable material from Isaiah in a way that illustrates, demonstrates, or aids in understanding the Scriptures.

9. Have students find the Scriptures in which each of the appearances and testimonies after the resurrection are found and put them in the correct order, with references (Evans does not include all the references, and some of the incidents he lists may not be familiar, such as "To the Apostles at Tiberias.") Use outside sources (commentaries, church historians, Church fathers) to support the order given.

This is not an exhaustive list of the verses, but each encounter has at least one verse. The teacher can have the students simply find all the rest of the verses. The teacher may disagree with Evans' order and have the student try to revise the chronology, or explain apparent discrepancies.

1. The women at the grave see the vision of angels (Matthew 28:5, Mark 16:5, Luke 24:4, John 20:12)

2. The women separate at the grave to make known the news --Mary Magdalene going to tell Peter and John, (John 20:2) who doubtless lived close by (for it seems that they reached the grave in a single run). The other women go to tell the other disciples who, probably, were at Bethany (Matthew 28:8).

3. Peter and John, hearing the news, run to the grave, leaving Mary. They then return home. (John 20:2 ff)

4. Mary follows; lingers at the grave; gets vision of the Master, and command to go tell the disciples. (John 20:18)

5. The other women see Christ on the way. (Mark 16:7)

6. Christ appears to the two on the way to Emmaus. (Luke 24:15 ff)

7. To Simon Peter. (Luke 24:34)

8. To the ten apostles, and other friends. (John 20:19 ff)

9. To the apostles at Tiberias (The Sea of Tiberias, where they went fishing) (John 21:1).

10. To the apostles and multitude on the mount. (Matthew 28:16)

11. To the disciples and friends at the ascension. (Luke 24:50)

12. To James (1 Cor. 15:7).

13. To Paul (1 Cor. 15:8).

10. Evans quotes Louis Agassiz, a 19th century scientist proficient in many fields. “No single instance has yet been adduced of the transformation of one animal species into another, either by natural or artificial selection; much less has it been demonstrated that the body of the brute has ever been developed into that of the man. The links that should bind man to the monkey have not been found. Not a single one can be shown. None have been found that stood nearer the monkey than the man of today.” Research the life and works of Agassiz and explain how he relied on facts and evidence and still rejected the evolutionary theories becoming popular in his time.

One source on Agassiz http://www.ucmp.berkeley.edu/history/agassiz.html contains the following quote: “Agassiz was no evolutionist; in fact, he was probably the last reputable scientist to reject evolution outright for any length of time after the publication of The Origin of Species.” This outrageous statement is typical of the treatment of scientists who retain belief in God and Creation. The writer is forced to acknowledge Agassiz as a scientist because his work in so many fields laid the foundation of many modern theories and practices, even evolutionary ones. The truth is that Darwinists had to twist Agassiz's works to fit their mold, and many erroneous theories, like that of Haeckel also mentioned in the article above, came out of this twisting. Modern scientists who question Evolution or consider the possibility of Intelligent Design are attacked, blacklisted and ridiculed. our website contains a great deal of information on reputable scientists who dare to question the Darwinian dogma. Answers in Genesis, the Discovery Institute, and Institute for Creation Research

11. Evans mentions "The Pelagian Theory" in his discussion of the effects of the fall, saying that the theory that Adam's sin affected him only and that man is perfectly well is part of that theory. Research and discuss Pelagius himself, the author of this theory, and find church fathers and historians who dealt with this heresy and refuted his claims. Also research and discuss the "semi-Pelagian" theory.

Pelagius (ca. AD 354 – ca. AD 420/440) lived a life of self-denial (asceticism) and believed in keeping the law and performing good works without God's help. He did not believe in original sin. Augustine of Hippo particularly opposed him. Pelagius was declared a heretic by the Council of Carthage.

12.Evans makes an excellent point about the supposed contradiction between Paul and James' views on faith and works. (II. The Definition of Faith 3. The Relation of Faith to works). Write your own essay on this subject, using Scriptures and commentaries to support your position.

There is no contradiction between Paul and James touching the matter of faith and works (cf. James 2:14-26; Rom. 4:1-12). Paul is looking at the matter from the Godward side, and asserts that we are justified, in the sight of God, meritoriously, without absolutely any works on our part. James considers the matter from the manward side, and asserts that we are justified, in the sight of man, evidentially, by works, and not by faith alone (2:24). In James it is not the ground of justification, as in Paul, but the demonstration. See under Justification, II. 4, p. 159.

13. Research and comment on Evans' position that Adoption was a Roman concept and not a Jewish one.

It will not seem so surprising to the student once he recalls and better understands the structure of the two societies. Remember that Romans bought and sold, conquered and divided, exchanged and traded their property with relative freedom, and also mingled freely with many other cultures and people groups as they gained control of other lands. This was not the case with Jews. The Law commanded that land given to a tribe/clan/family always remain with them, even if temporarily leased until the year of the Jubilee. In a case where a man with children died, a relative might take in the children but they would return to their father's inheritance, not step into their surrogate family's. Family structure among the Jews was much broader and there was nearly always a true relative to inherit, making any kind of adoption not only unnecessary but also contrary to the Law. The Jews were also supposed to remain distinct from the Gentiles due to the dangers of idolatry and moral pollution, so the only Gentiles admitted into their society would be proselytes. Proselytes might properly be considered "adopted," and students can research the possibility that they were given land and/or included as part of some tribe or clan at any time during Israel's history.

14. Evans creates a kind of "prayer diary" showing progression in Abraham's prayer life. Have students attempt to create such a diary for another Bible person, for example, Jacob, Moses, Miriam, David, Esther, Mary, Jesus, or Paul. Have the student research to develop a list of Scriptures and commentary similar to what Evans does with Abraham, including as many as possible of the major types of prayer he gives (conversation or dialogue,

intercession, personal, blessings). Later Evans also says, "True prayer consists of such elements as adoration, praise, petition, pleading, thanksgiving, intercession, communion, waiting." Consider including examples of these as well.

This assignment will produce many possible results. It is not necessary to quote exact verses of a person's speech, but to include Scriptures that deal with the person's attitude toward and relationship with God, possibly as observed by other people or God Himself. It may be necessary to combine a number of women's prayer experiences in one diary since we are not given many such examples in the Scriptures.

15. Evans briefly discusses "Universal Christian Inspiration (or Illumination)." Research to learn what groups hold to this teaching. Evans says, "If this be the true view, there seems to be no plausible reason why a new Bible should not be possible to-day. And yet no individual, however extreme his claims to inspiration may be, has even ventured such a task."

Although we agree that no other Christian writings hold a true claim to Inspiration, this statement of Evans' is not strictly true. We have the writings known as the Book of Mormon, The Pearl of Great Price, and the massive writings of the Roman Catholic Church, just to name a few, which do purport to be as authoritative as Scripture for Christians. Explain why these writings do not meet the standard of Inspiration.

16. Evans spends considerable time explaining why the RV translation of II Timothy 3:16 is wrong and why it is important to make this point clear. Many people have rejected the RV translation as a whole because of this error. Research commentaries and Bible scholars, as well as some of the people Evans quotes in his discussion on this point, and expand upon the argument that this translation of this verse is erroneous, hypocritical and dangerous.

The Revised Version translation of 2 Tim. 3:16 is erroneous. The reader might infer from it that there is some Scripture that is not inspired. If Paul had said, "All Scripture that is divinely inspired is also profitable, etc.," he would virtually have said, "There is some Scripture, some part of the Bible, that is not profitable, etc., and therefore is not inspired." This is what the spirit of rationalism wants, namely, to make human reason the test and judge and measure of what is inspired and what is not. One man says such and such a verse is not profitable to him, another says such and such a verse is not profitable to him; a third says such and such is not profitable to him. The result is that no Bible is left.

17. Evans points out that the words "God said" occur ten times in the first chapter of Genesis alone. Write an essay explaining how this reinforces the authority of the literal nature of the account of Creation. Compare it with some of the other examples from Scripture where the authority of the Word is reinforced by statements such as "God said," or "The Word of the Lord came ... saying."

Examples include the Flood and how Noah is spoken of in other Scriptures as preaching righteousness and warning the people, the plagues on Egypt, fulfilled prophecy in the Life of Christ, and the fear of unbelievers when faced with proofs of the authority of God's Word (Jericho, the miracles of Peter and Paul).

18. Evans explains his position on how Inspiration affected the actual words used to write the Scriptures. Using commentaries and scholarly sources, explain where you agree or disagree with his position and state your own position on this subject based on your research. Note that in this section he does not present any Scriptural proofs. Is this because he considers this a summary of the evidence he has already presented? Are the Scriptures he has presented sufficient or can you add more to support your own position?

II. THE INSPIRATION OF THE BIBLE.

5. WHAT IS THE NATURE OF THE INSPIRATION THAT CHARACTERIZED THE WRITERS OF THE SCRIPTURES, AND IN WHAT DEGREE WERE THEY UNDER ITS INFLUENCE?

19. Evans quotes Joseph Parker, a Nonconformist preacher in England in the 1800's. Research what it meant to be a "Nonconformist" in England in this time period (it does not mean simply unconventional or independent). The student may also research and write about Joseph Parker himself, who was a popular preacher in his time, expressed strong opinions about truth, faith and character, and was known for being unconventional.

http://chrisfieldblog.com/2009/04/09/joseph-parker

Protestant Nonconformist Texts: The nineteenth century By Robert Tudur Jones, Alan P. F. Sell, David William Bebbington, Kenneth Dix, Alan Ruston is available on Google Books and includes a section on Parker.

20. Research Evans' statements about the prevalence of the doctrine of the Second Coming:

"It is claimed that one out of every thirty verses in the Bible mentions this doctrine; to every one mention of the first coming the second coming is mentioned eight times; 318 references to it are made in 216 chapters." Be sure to look for instances where the first and second comings may be combined. The student may discuss the perspectives in Jesus' time where they spoke of "the Prophet," their views on who and what the Messiah would be, and what if any, position Jews take on the Second Coming today.

http://bibleprophesy.org/15differences.htm is one possible place to start research.

21. Research the differences between the beliefs of the Sadducees and Pharisees. Especially include positions on

spiritual versus material issues and the resurrection of the dead. Student may also discuss what Jews in recent or modern times believe about the Messiah, the afterlife, and the restoration of temple worship. Keep in mind that there are many sects of Judaism, as there are of Christianity. Some to investigate are Hassidic, "Observant" Jews, Reformed Jews, and Secular Jews.

http://www.jewishvirtuallibrary.org/jsource/History/sadduceespharisees essenes.html is one possible place to start research.

Ruth

The Slow of Heart Bible Study Series Part One

"Oh, fools, and slow of heart, to believe all that the prophets have spoken: ought not Christ have suffered these things and to enter into His glory? and beginning at Moses and all the prophets he expounded unto them in all the scriptures the things concerning Himself."

With Commentary by the Anything Box Puppets

Ruth: The Slow of Heart Bible Study Series, Part One

"Oh, fools, and slow of heart, to believe all that the prophets have spoken: ought not Christ have suffered these things and to enter into His glory? and beginning at Moses and all the prophets he expounded unto them in all the scriptures the things concerning Himself."
Luke 24:25-26

With Commentary by the Anything Box Puppets

The Slow of Heart series is designed around the frame tale of Jesus meeting the disciples on the road to Emmaus. Jesus started at Moses and told them how the Scriptures taught about Him and revealed everything about Him.

This version of Ruth is designed to give a complete, accurate account of the biblical narrative and as a study guide for younger readers. It is a companion to a set of videos available free on YouTube.

https://www.youtube.com/@ffvp5657

Study questions are included at the end. The student should read the book of Ruth in the Bible as well as this study version.

Prologue –On the Road to Emmaus

Two men walked along the dusty road to Emmaus.

"We did not understand," one said. "He knew He was going to die. He told us it would happen, remember?"

"There were so many things we did not understand, Thaddeus," said his friend, whose name was Cleopas, "about the kingdom, about how we should live -- about heaven."

"Hello, friends. May I join you? What are you talking about?"

The two men turned in surprise as a stranger came up behind them. It was he who had spoken.

"Have you heard nothing about all that has happened in Jerusalem these past few days?" Cleopas asked.

"Tell me," the stranger said.

"Jesus of Nazareth, the one who was such a mighty prophet, has been killed," Thaddeus explained. "Our rulers and priests turned him over to the Romans and they crucified him."

"That was three days ago," Cleopas told the stranger. "But some of our friends who followed him have told us that they have seen him alive."

“Foolish fellows,” the stranger said, shaking his head. “These things had to happen to Jesus-- His suffering was foretold by the prophets. From the time of Moses -- all through the scriptures it is told. Remember Ruth?”

“Ruth? What about Ruth?” Cleopas asked.

“Wait! Ruth!” cried Thaddeus. “Ruth was the Moabitess who came into the line of the House of David by marrying Boaz.’“

“‘Ruth started out with a lot of troubles,’“ nodded Cleopas. “I remember that too.”

“We had hoped that Jesus was the one who was going to redeem Israel, like Boaz redeemed Ruth,” Thaddeus said sadly.

“But what has Ruth got to do with the death of our Lord?” Cleopas asked the stranger.

The stranger replied, “Remember what Jesus said? ‘When these things begin to take place, stand up and lift up your heads, because your redemption is drawing near.’ “

“Ruth ... Ruth ... I remember we were told about the old prophetess who lived in the temple at the time of Jesus’ birth. She gave thanks to God and spoke about the child to all who were looking forward to the redemption of Jerusalem.”

“I do seem to remember something like that,” Thaddeus nodded.

“‘All men will hate you because of me,” said the stranger, “‘but he who stands firm to the end will be saved.’“

“But what are we waiting for? What will the end be?” Cleopas said.

“Listen to the story of Ruth. I’ll tell it as we walk,” the stranger suggested. “In the days when the Judges ruled ”

Chapter One -- A Famine and a Family

In the days when the judges ruled God's people there was a famine in the land of Israel. A man from Bethlehem Judah, named Elimelech, took his wife, Naomi, and his two sons, Mahlon and Chilion, and went to stay in the land of Moab.

Elimelech, Naomi's husband, died. She was left with her two sons. The two sons took wives from the women of Moab. One was called Orpah, and the other, Ruth.

They lived there about ten years, and Mahlon and Chilion both died. Naomi was left without her husband or her two sons.

Naomi heard in the country of Moab that the Lord had given His people bread. So she set out from Moab to return to Judah, and her daughters-in-law went along with her on the way.

"Go back to your mothers' houses, each of you," Naomi said to her daughters-in-law. "The Lord treat you kindly, just as you have treated me, and my sons who have died. The Lord allow you to find rest, each in the house of another husband. She kissed them, and all of them began to cry.

"We will return with you to your people," Ruth and Orpah said to Naomi.

"Turn back, my daughters," Naomi told them. "Why should you come with me? Am I going to give birth to more sons, so that you could marry them? Go your ways. I am too old to have a husband. Even if I had a husband tonight, and sons, would you wait until they have grown up? Would you keep from having husbands for their sakes? No, my daughters. It makes me very sad for your sakes that the Lord has done this to me."

They all began to cry again, and Orpah kissed her mother-in-law and left, but Ruth held on to her. Naomi said to Ruth, "Look, your sister-in-law had gone back to her people, and her gods. Return like she has."

"Don't ask me to leave you," Ruth said. "Don't ask me to return from following after you. Where you go, I will go. Where you live, I will live. Your people will be my people, and your God my God. Where you die, I will die, and be buried there. The Lord do as much to me, and even more, if anything but death separates you from me."

When Naomi saw that Ruth's mind was made up, she stopped talking to her. So the two of them went on until they came to Bethlehem. The whole city was stirred up when they arrived.

"Is this Naomi?" The people asked.

"Do not call me Naomi," Naomi told them. "Call me Mara. The Almighty has treated me very bitterly. I went out full, and the Lord brought me home empty. Why call me Naomi, the pleasant one, when you can see that the Lord has spoken against me, and punished me?"

So Naomi returned, and Ruth, the Moabitess, her daughter-in-law with her. They came to Bethlehem at the beginning of the barley harvest.

Chapter Two – Bitterness and Barley

Ruth said to Naomi, "Let me go to the fields and glean grain after someone who will show me kindness."

"Go, my daughter," Naomi said. Ruth went, and gleaned after the reapers. Naomi had a close relative, a powerful man, and very rich, a member of Elimelech's family. His name was Boaz. Ruth happened to come to a field that belonged to Boaz, Elimelech's relative.

Boaz came from Bethlehem and said to his reapers, "The Lord be with you." They answered, "The Lord bless you!"

"Whose young woman is that?" Boaz asked the foreman of the reapers. The foreman told him, "It is the young woman from Moab, who came back with Naomi. She said, 'Please let me glean and gather grain after the reapers among the sheaves.' She came, and she has worked since early morning, except for a little rest in the shelter."

"Listen to me, my daughter," Boaz said to Ruth. "Do not go to glean in another field. Do not leave here. Remain right with my young women. Keep your eyes on the field they reap. Go right after them. Haven't I ordered the young men not to touch you? When you are thirsty, go to the pots of water the young men have drawn and drink from them."

Ruth fell down on her face and bowed to the ground. "Why have you chosen to notice me, and show me kindness, since I am a foreigner?"

"I have been told about everything you have done for your mother-in-law since the death of your husband," Boaz explained. "I know how you left your father and mother, and the land where you were born, and came to a people you never knew before. The Lord God of Israel reward you greatly for your good work, since you have come to trust under His wings."

"Let me continue to know your kindness," Ruth said to Boaz. "You have comforted me, and spoken in a friendly way to your servant, even though I am not as important as one of your young women."

"At mealtime come here," Boaz told Ruth. "Eat of the bread, and dip your piece in the vinegar." She sat beside the reapers. Boaz reached her roasted grain, and she ate, and had more than enough. She left, and went back to her gleaning.

"Let her glean right in the sheaves," Boaz told his young men. "Don't chase her away. Let fall some handfuls on purpose for her. Leave them for her to pick up, and do not forbid her."

Ruth gleaned in the field until evening, and then beat out what she had gleaned, a large basket full of grain. She picked it up, returned to the city, and showed her mother-in-law what she had gleaned. She also gave Naomi the food she had left over from what Boaz had given her.

"Where did you glean today, my daughter?" Naomi gasped. "The Lord bless the man who noticed you."

"The man's name is Boaz," Ruth told her mother-in-law.

"The Lord bless him indeed," Naomi exclaimed. "The Lord hasn't stopped showing kindness to the living and the dead. This man is a very close relative."

"He also told me to stay close by his young men until the end of all the harvest," Ruth explained.

"That is good, my daughter," Naomi said. "Go out with his young women, and don't let anyone find you in another field." So Ruth stayed close by Boaz's young women until the end of the barley and wheat harvests. She lived with her mother-in-law.

Chapter Three -- A Midnight Visitor

"I am going to find rest for you, my daughter," Naomi said to Ruth. "I am going to make sure all is well with you. Boaz, whose young women you worked beside, is a close relative of ours, as I told you before. He is going to winnow barley at the threshing floor tonight.

"Wash yourself, and put on your perfume and your best dress, and go down to the threshing floor. Do not make yourself known to the man until he is done eating and drinking. When he lies down, notice the place where he is. Go in, uncover his feet, and lie down. He will tell you what to do next."

“I will do everything you have told me,” Ruth said.

Ruth went down to the threshing floor, and did exactly what Naomi had told her. After Boaz had eaten and drunk, and he was happy, he went to lie down at the foot of the grain pile. Ruth came quietly, uncovered his feet, and lay down.

At midnight Boaz was frightened. He sat up and saw a woman lying at his feet. “Who are you?” he demanded.

“I am Ruth, your servant,” Ruth answered. “Spread your robe over your servant, because you are a close relative.”

“The Lord bless you, my daughter,” smiled Boaz. “You have been more kind now than at the beginning. You didn’t follow young men, whether they were rich or poor. Do not be afraid, my daughter. I will do everything you need. All the people in my city know you are a pure young woman. It is true that I am a near kinsman, but there is one nearer than I am. Stay here tonight. In the morning, if he will do the relative’s duty for you, all right. If he won’t, then I will, as the Lord lives. Lie down until morning.”

Ruth lay at his feet until early morning, and she got up before it was light enough to see who was there. Boaz said, “Don’t let people know a woman came to the threshing floor. Bring the shawl you are wearing here. Hold it up.” Boaz gave her six measures of barley in her shawl.

“Don’t go home to your mother-in-law empty-handed.”

Ruth returned to the city. When she came to Naomi, her mother-in-law asked, “Did things go well?” Ruth told her all that had happened, and showed her the barley Boaz had given her.

“He told me not to come home to you empty-handed,” Ruth explained.

"Rest, my daughter," Naomi told her. "You'll soon know how the matter will turn out. Boaz won't rest until he's settled everything today."

Chapter Four –The Kinsman-Redeemers

Boaz went up to the city gate and sat down. The relative he had told Ruth about came by. Boaz said, "Hello, cousin. Come here and sit down." He also took ten men of the elders of the city and said, "Sit down here." They sat down.

"Naomi, who came back from Moab, is selling a piece of land that belonged to Elimelech, our relative. I thought I should tell you, so that you can buy it before the elders of our people. If you will redeem it, redeem it. But if you won't, tell me, so I will know. There is no one else besides you and me to redeem it, and I am after you."

"I will redeem it," the relative replied.

"On the day you buy the field from Naomi," Boaz added, "You must also buy it from Ruth, the Moabitess, the wife of the dead, to have children in the dead man's name to keep his inheritance alive."

"I cannot redeem it," the kinsman said. "I might harm my own inheritance. Redeem it for yourself, because I can't."

It was the custom in Israel when people redeemed or exchanged something, that when a man wanted to confirm something, he took off his shoe, and gave it to his neighbor as a symbol. So the relative took off his shoe and gave it to Boaz. "Buy it for yourself," he said.

"You are witnesses today," Boaz said to all the elders and people gathered there, "That I have bought all that was Elimelech's, and all that was Chilion's and Mahlon's, from Naomi. I have also bought Ruth, the Moabitess, to be my wife. She was the wife of Mahlon, and we will raise up children in his name, to keep his inheritance from disappearing in Israel. You are witnesses of all this."

"We are witnesses," the elders and the people said to Boaz. "The Lord make this woman coming into your house like Rachel and Leah, who together made the whole nation of Israel. Do well in Ephrathah, and be famous in Bethlehem. Let your house be like the house of Pharez, the son of Judah and Tamar, from the children this young woman will give you."

So Boaz took Ruth, and she became his wife. The Lord gave them a son. The women said to Naomi, "Praise the Lord, Who has given you a relative today, and will make his name famous in Israel. He will give you back your life, and care for you in your old age. Your daughter-in-law, who loves you, and who is better to you than seven sons, has given birth to him."

Naomi took the child, and put it to her breast, and became its nurse. The women who were Naomi's neighbors gave him a name. "A son is born to Naomi," they said. They called his name Obed. He is the father of Jesse, the father of David.

Epilogue -- Dinner in Emmaus

Cleopas and Thaddeus were startled to realize that they had arrived at the house in Emmaus as the stranger finished talking. The storyteller started to go on his way, but the two friends told him he must stay and have dinner with them.

"What was it about Ruth that the Lord was trying to tell us?" Cleopas asked.

"Ruth needed someone to save her," Thaddeus said thoughtfully. Cleopas nodded.

"Ruth gave up everything, just like we did," Thaddeus said sadly.

"I don't think that's what the Lord wanted us to understand about her, though," Cleopas frowned.

"No. It's something to do with redemption," Thaddeus insisted. "He said our redemption was near."

"Ruth had to work and wait before she was redeemed."

"Maybe that's it. Maybe if we just wait, we'll understand what's going to happen."

"Come. It is time to give thanks," the stranger broke in as they sat down at the table. He prayed for the food and reached for the basket of bread.

"Your redemption draws nigh ... your redemption draws nigh ..."

Thaddeus reached out his hand for the bread the stranger held out to him. Suddenly both Cleopas and Thaddeus stared in amazement.

"It is the Lord!" They both shouted together. "He is alive!"

As quickly as they spoke the words, Jesus vanished.

"The Lord died to redeem us!" shouted Cleopas.

"Jesus is our kinsman-redeemer! He paid the price to buy us from death by dying Himself!"

"He is alive! Thaddeus! Thaddeus! We should have known it was Him. The way He taught the Scriptures -- "

"I know! It made my heart burn within me!"

"Mine too. I remember something else the Lord said."

"What? More about Ruth?"

"No. Not about Ruth. He told you at the Last Supper. 'Because I live, you shall live also.'"

"Because He lives, we shall live also! That's what He was trying to tell us. Believe, and live! Live forever!"

Grampa

Ruth Commentary by the Anything Box Characters

Jerry: Why is Ruth's story so important?

Gloria: Actually, it's Naomi's story.

Jerry: Ok ... Well, it's a nice story, and it is a part of the Bible, but why's it so important?

Grampa: One of the most important works Christ did was to redeem all mankind. Ruth is the most beautiful, clear illustration of this redemption in all the Word of God. Ruth is a Gentile, with no rights to the promises of God. Her faith and obedience to the Word of God is an example that all Gentiles as the Bride of Christ should strive for.

Everyone knows that she worked hard, but very few people understand how hard she worked. Ruth gleaned all day, that is, picked up individual stalks of grain that the reapers dropped, then she threshed the grain the same day. Threshing the grain is probably as difficult as gleaning, but faster. When Ruth finished threshing, she had about an ephah of barley. Now that doesn't mean much to us because we don't know what an ephah is. Well, an ephah's at least 20 liters, maybe as many as 35. For those of you not familiar with liters, that's at least five and a quarter gallons, and maybe as much as nine and a quarter gallons. Another way of saying the same thing is, about a bushel. That's a bushel after threshing, not before.

Jerry: Whoa! That sure is a lot of work, but what does Ruth have to do with our redemption?

Gloria: Ruth is, like we are, Gentiles, without the promises of God, and Boaz is, like God, buying us back when we had no hope.

Grampa: Actually, Naomi was the one redeemed. Ruth married into the family of Elimelech, so she was just part of the deal. According to the law, Elimelech's property still belonged to Elimelech, even though he was dead. Naomi and Ruth were part of that property. Under Mosaic law, the land could never be sold. However, someone else had taken the property while Elimelech was gone, and whoever held it had the right to be paid. That payment to restore the land to the rightful owner was the redemption price. However, the relative who redeemed the property also had the obligation to take care of Ruth and Naomi as well as take the land. This obligation meant take Ruth as your own wife. So if Boaz had sons by another wife, his sons would receive his land and Ruth's sons would receive Elimelech's land. If the only sons Boaz had were by Ruth, they would inherit all the land.

Jerry: So who does God pay off?

Gloria: Excuse me?

Jerry: Grampa said that Jesus redeemed us and that redemption is paying the redemption price to the man who had the land at the time. So who did God pay to get us?

Grampa: Heh heh heh. If you are really serious, Paul answers that question in great detail in the books of Romans and Galatians. The Bible says that we are born in unbelief and spiritual darkness in the kingdom of

Satan. We are born children under the law in the slave market of sin.

Gloria: So God ... had to ... pay off Satan?

Grampa: There are believers who teach that. What the Word of God is very clear about, however, is that Christ came to redeem those under the law. The redemption price was God's holy requirement of His law. That price was the death on the tree of the sinless substitute, Jesus the Messiah.

Jerry: So God had to pay off Himself?

Gloria: Since we are all sinners, there is nothing we can offer to meet the just and holy requirements of a just and holy God.

Grampa: Yes, the Bible is very clear about that.

Gloria: So ... Ruth represents the church ...

Grampa: And every other believer since Adam ...

Jerry: And Boaz pictures God, paying a price that Ruth and Naomi could never pay.

Grampa: That's very good. Just remember, even though Ruth and Boaz are very good, very clear pictures of redemption, they are only pictures.

Gloria: Ruth's children were still sinners ...

Jerry: and Ruth worked hard to make Boaz want her. That would picture working for our salvation.

Grampa: Very good. We know that God's word teaches us that salvation is a free gift, so even though we are to give our all to Jesus, we work because we are saved, not to become saved.

Jerry: thanks, Grampa. I've got to read Ruth again. Ruth really is a very important book of the Bible.

Study Questions and Answers for Ruth

1. What other book in the Bible is set at the same time as Ruth? *Judges*

2. Why did Elimelech take his family away from Israel? *a famine*

3. What country did they go to? *Moab*

4. What did Mahlon and Chilion do there? *married Moabite women*

5. What happened to Elimelech, Mahlon and Chilion? *they died*

6. What news did Naomi hear that made her decide to return to Israel? *the famine was over*

7. What did she tell Ruth and Orpah to do when they wanted to come with her? *go back to your people and your gods*

8. What did Orpah do? *went back*

9. What did Ruth do? *promised to stay with Naomi, to be part of her people and serve God*

10. What did Naomi change her name to, and what was the meaning of the new name? *Mara, bitterness*

11. What did Ruth do to get food? *went out and gleaned in a field*

12. Whose field was it? *Boaz's*

13. Why was Boaz kind to Ruth? (two reasons) *because he had heard how good she was to Naomi, and that she had left her own people to serve the true God*

14. What instructions did Boaz give Ruth? *Don't go glean anywhere else, stay with his maidens.*

15. What instructions did he give his workers? (3 possible answers) *Don't harm her, let her glean right among the sheaves, let grain fall for her on purpose.*

16. How much was Ruth able to glean that day? *an ephah of barley*

17. What did Naomi tell Ruth about Boaz? (two things) *he was blessed for taking notice of Ruth, and he was a close relative*

18. What was Naomi's plan to secure Ruth's future? *Ruth was to ask for Boaz's protection as a close relative, to get him to redeem her, Naomi and their land*

19. What did Boaz say had to be done first? *A closer relative had to be asked first if he wanted to redeem the property*

20. How did Boaz prepare to ask the closer relative? *Came to the city gate and got ten witnesses*

21. Did the relative agree to redeem the land? *yes, at first*

22. What did Boaz tell him that made him change his mind? *He reminded him that he would have to marry*

Ruth, since she was the widow of Mahlon, Elimelech's son, and whoever got the land would have to raise up sons in Elimelech/Mahlon's name according to the law of Moses

24. How did they "seal the bargain" that Boaz would become the redeemer? *the other relative took off his shoe*

25. What was the name of the child Ruth and Boaz had after their marriage? *Obed*

26. What did people say about the child? *Naomi has a son*

27. What did they say about Ruth? *She was better to Naomi than seven sons*

28. What two famous people are descended from Ruth and Boaz? *David and Jesus Christ*

30. Why is the story of Ruth important? *it pictures redemption*

31. Give two examples of the hard work Ruth had to perform. *gleaning (picking up dropped grain after reapers all day) threshing (beating out the heads of grain from the stalks at the end of the long day of gleaning)*

32. How much threshed grain did she get in modern terms? *20-35 liters or 5 1/4 to 9 1/4 gallons, or about a bushel.*

33. Why is redemption so important as illustrated by the case of Ruth and Naomi? *Elimelech's land was maintained by someone else. That person had to be paid for his expense of caring for the land before Naomi could get the land back. Ruth and Naomi had no money to pay to redeem the land, so Boaz had to pay the price for them. Without him they had no hope.*

34. Did God pay Satan to redeem us from sin? *Christ came to redeem those under the law who had*

become slaves to sin and had no hope of saving themselves. The redemption price was God's holy requirement of His law. That price was the death on the tree of the sinless substitute, Jesus the Messiah. It was paid to satisfy God's law, not to satisfy Satan.

35. Ruth's hard work impressed Boaz and led him to redeem her. Since Ruth is a picture of redemption, does that mean we have to work to be redeemed?
No. No matter how hard Ruth worked she still couldn't do enough to redeem herself and Naomi. Boaz had to do what she had no power or hope of doing herself, just as Jesus Christ did what we had no power to do ourselves.

Optional research, essay, or project questions for Ruth.

(If the students studying the book are not old enough to read and do research themselves the teacher can ignore the following, or choose to do this as a "team project" with the teacher or older students who can help.

1. God gave commandments in the law concerning foreigners coming to live in Israel. Research to find what a foreigner needed to do. Find specific references to God permitting the marrying foreign wives and how Moab and its people were normally to be treated.

2. Research and report on the process of harvesting and processing wheat and barley in the times before machinery was available (or in third-world places today). Describe how it was done, what animals or equipment was available, and how many hours it might take to thresh out a bushel of barley (Remember, too, that bread or something cooked had to be made out of the barley after Ruth got home, and discuss that as well.)

3. Create a diorama or drawing/painting of what Bethlehem may have looked like, where the fields may have been in relation to where Naomi and Ruth lived, showing how much distance Ruth would have had to walk back and forth each day, and the ground she might have covered while working.

4. Create a map of Moab and Israel showing travel routes, where Bethlehem was located, and try to determine some towns or cities where the family might have lived in Moab.

5. Research the customs of property and personal redemption/exchange based on the Scriptures and Bible commentaries. Take into account the law covering when a man refused to marry a woman to carry on his brother's name (which mentions the shoe custom), the Year of Jubilee, and laws covering Israelite bondservants.

Study Guide for the Book of Proverbs

This study is based on the KJV Bible.

Edward Poynter 1890 The Visit of the Queen of Sheba to King Solomon Art Gallery of New South Wales Wikimedia Commons Public Domain

Study Guide for the Book of Proverbs

This study is based on the KJV Bible. Some questions and answers are paraphrased. Each assignment is built around a chapter. Most questions are short answer or fill in the blank. Some sections have one or more essay assignments. It is up to the teacher to decide how long to spend on each chapter and whether or not to assign the essay question, how long the finished essay should be, and whether it should include research outside the passage.)

Assignment One: Read Ch. 1

Assignment One: Read Chapter 1

1. Who wrote most of the Proverbs? *Solomon*

2. List three things studying Proverbs can provide (1: 2-4) *instruction, wisdom, knowledge, understanding (perception), justice, judgment, equity, discernment (subtlety) are all possible answers*

3. List two responses of a wise man to Proverbs. (vv.5-6) *hearing, learning, understanding, taking good advice*

4. The of the Lord is the beginning of knowledge and despise wisdom and instruction. *fear, fools*

5. What does Proverbs tell us to do concerning our parents and their teaching? *hear, do not forsake*

6. For they shall be an of grace unto thy head, and about thy neck. *ornament, chains*

Necklace in ancient style

7. Verses 10-19 describe being tempted to join groups of thieves and murderers. It might seem obvious that we are to avoid the company of such people, but the news is full of the young committing crimes in groups, sometimes openly, attacking individuals or stores, injuring or killing people for no apparent reason. Write an essay paraphrasing these verses and describing the wrong behavior, the warnings of consequences, and how these people ignore them.

Some possible answers should include evidences of peer pressure and how it leads to escalating wrong behavior. Gangs put a premium on a distorted sense of "respect" enforced by fear, violence to enhance their power over others. The promise of monetary gain can be a great temptation if young people see themselves as poor, lacking things others have, or if they are jealous of others' prosperity. Sharing equally in the spoils is a tempting concept. It is important to realize that these are not friendships, games or entertainment. They are criminal conspiracies. The Scriptures teach that people will fight back and avoid attempts by these wrongdoers, and that the plans can backfire.

8. (vv. 20-21) Wisdom is spoken of as crying, speaking, being in the streets, at the gates, in the chief places, so

that no one can her message.
Ignore

9. (v. 22) What are three things Wisdom accuses people of being?
Possible answers: simple, loving simplicity, scorners, fools, haters of knowledge

10. (v. 23) Wisdom reproves, turning her hearers so she can .
teach them, make them able to learn and understand

11. (vv. 24-27) Calamity comes to those who wisdom's call and her counsel.
refuse, ignore

12. (vv. 28-31) Give one reason why wisdom refuses to help those who call on her.
two possible answers: they hated knowledge, did not choose to fear the Lord

13. (vv. 32-33) What is the penalty for ignoring wisdom?
death, destruction

14. What is one reward for listening?
dwelling safely, no fear of evil

Assignment Two: Read Ch. 2

Assignment Two: Read Ch. 2

1. " my words, my commandments ... thine ear ... thine heart to understanding."
receive, hide, incline, apply

2. Cry after , lift up your voice for , seek her as search for her as for treasures.
knowledge, understanding, silver, hid

3. Where does wisdom come from?
the Lord

4. Who does the Lord store up wisdom for?
the righteous

5. Wisdom will enter your and knowledge will be to your soul.
heart, pleasant

6. shall preserve you, understanding shall you.
Discretion, keep

7. Wisdom will protect you from the man and deliver you from the woman.
evil, strange

Painting of wayward woman

8. Write an essay giving some details about the evil man and the strange woman described in Proverbs 2: 12-19 that can be used as clues to identify these people in modern life.
Their speech betrays them (crude or foul language), they prefer darkness (sunglasses to be "cool," night activities,) they admire evildoers (mobsters, gang members, antiheroes), say insincere things to make you feel good, rude to or contradicting adults, antagonistic toward the Bible and church, obsessed with death (vampires, skulls), self-destructive behavior (body mutilation, drug abuse).

Assignment Three: Read Ch. 3

Assignment Three: Read Ch. 3

1. What two things can result from remembering God's commands?
long life, peace

2. Keep and bound around your neck and written on your heart.
mercy, truth

3.What should you not lean on?
your own understanding

4. What is a phrase that means to be falsely proud or self-sufficient?
wise in your own eyes

5. Prosperity can be one of the visible rewards of .
honoring the Lord

6. Why should you not be angry when God disciplines you?
it shows His love

7. Wisdom is better than what three precious things?
silver, gold, rubies

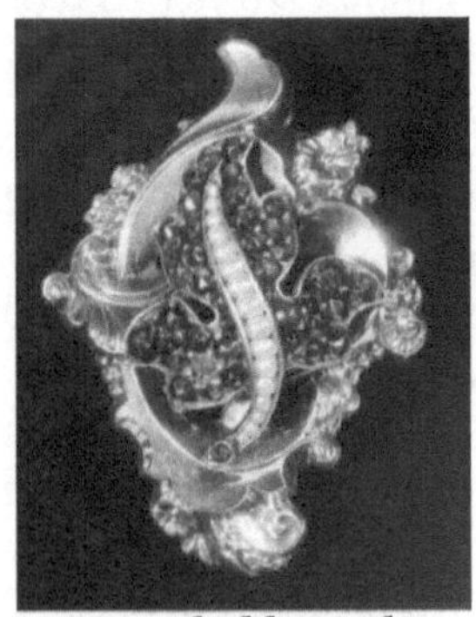

Jeweled brooch

8. List three benefits of seeking wisdom.
possible answers: life, riches, honor, pleasantness, peace, happiness

9. Wisdom, understanding and knowledge were necessary to God in creating and "operating" the world. Name three things man needs wisdom to do in the world?
Possible answers are: live, get God's grace, have safety, walk without stumbling, sleep peacefully

10. Two things you should not do to neighbors are
withhold good, devise evil

11. Choose one of the following pairs of people and write an essay contrasting their behavior, God's attitude toward them, and their futures. a) oppressor vs just b) scorner vs lowly fools vs wise
In each case, the wicked is self-centered, does things to enrich himself at the expense of others, and is under God's judgment. The good example knows God's Word, advances righteousness and seeks the good of others, and is blessed by God. The future of the wicked is being overthrown and destroyed. The future of the righteous is rewarded by God.

Assignment Four: Read Ch. 4

Assignment Four: Read Ch. 4

1. Where did the father in Chapter 4 get his teaching?
his father

2. What are two symbols of honor that are both physical and spiritual mentioned as being given by wisdom?
head-ornament of grace, crown of glory

Jeweled brooch

3. What are the food and drink of the wicked?
bread of wickedness, wine of violence

4. The path of the just is as the light, ... but the way of the wicked is as darkness. They know not at what they .
shining, stumble

5. List five body parts mentioned in connection with the self-control taught in Proverbs 4:20-27
ear, eyes, heart, mouth, lips, feet, (right hand, left hand, and flesh may also be possible answers)

Assignment Five: read Ch. 5

Assignment Five: Read Ch. 5

1. Study Chapter 5. Choose one of the three essay topics to write about.

a) Based on what Proverbs has taught so far, how do such things as wisdom, understanding and discretion help prevent physical sins and their consequences?

b) Discuss sexual sins based on this chapter's content. Contrast this to the world's view that sexual attraction is the same as love and can't be chosen or controlled. "It just happens."

c) Discuss sins that lead to dishonor and loss of reputation such as cheating, lying or addiction.

Punishing a truant in the 1800s – Tying a weight to his ankle.

Possible answers in each case should include that Proverbs teaches over and over the principles of thoroughly knowing God's Word, exercising control over every part of the body, listening to parents and obeying their teaching. These principles originate with God Himself and directed His very acts of creating and preserving the world, so they must apply to man living in the world as well. The reward for following these instructions is life, peace, health, honor, and the penalty for ignoring them is fear, stumbling, and death. Controlling your mind, heart, body, and all the rest, not just with vague "will power," but with God's power, will allow a person tempted to remember the duty to obey and the punishment for disobeying.

Assignment Six: read Ch. 6

Assignment Six: Read Ch. 6

1. What is it a great mistake to do?
co-signing a loan with a friend

2. Where should a sluggard go for a good example?
the ant

Sluggard

3. What does this example not need to get work done?
overseer or ruler

4. What can come quickly to a lazy person?
Poverty

5. A wicked man "deviseth continually: he soweth ."
evil, discord

6. List four of the character traits that the Lord hates.
pride, lying, murder, wicked imagination, running to mischief, false witness, sowing discord among brothers

7. The commandments or laws of parents are good to keep "when thou , ... [to] lead thee, when thou sleepest, ...[to] thee, and when thou wakest ... [to] with thee."
goest, keep, talk

8. The is a lamp ... to keep thee from the woman.
commandment, evil

9. Sexual sin can reduce a man to
a piece of bread

masked thief

10. A thief who steals for food is not , but if he is caught he must repay .
despised, sevenfold

11. You cannot wipe away the of adultery with gifts.
dishonor

Assignment Seven: read Ch. 7

Assignment Seven: Read Ch. 7

1. List three ways we should keep the commandments close to us.
as the apple of your eye, bound on your fingers, written on the tablet of your heart, calling wisdom your sister, calling understanding your relative

Adulteress/Prostitute

2. Write a short essay discussing the prostitute/adulteress. Use specific references to verses in the chapter. Consider the following questions: How does she tempt the young man? Does she lie to him? What is her personality like? Does she do/say anything to make him think they are not doing wrong?
v. 5, she flatters, v. 9, she waits for darkness, v. 10, she dresses to seduce and plans her sin carefully, v. 11, she is loud, stubborn, and will not stay home, v. 12, she prowls for prey, v. 13, she shows no restraint, v. 14, she pretends to be pure and obedient to the law, v. 15, claims to wait just for him, v. 16, 17, her bedroom is rich and attractive, v. 18 she calls what they will do love, v. 19-21 she assures him they will not get caught.

3. List three comparisons describing what will happen to those who go to the wicked woman.
ox to slaughter, fool to stocks, dart in liver, bird in snare

4. The evil woman has “cast down many and many men have been slain by her.”
wounded, strong

Assignment Eight: read Ch. 8

Assignment Eight: Read Ch. 4

Wisdom rejoicing in mankind

1. Write a short essay describing wisdom. Use specific references to verses in the chapter. Choose one or more of the following topics: Discuss how she tries to gather people to her. How does she convince people of how important her teaching is? How was wisdom involved in creation? What are the rewards/consequences of obeying/not obeying wisdom?
v.1-3 places where she goes to be heard v. 4-5, who she wants to speak to , v. 6-8 description of what she speaks, v. 9, who can understand them, v. 10-11 the value of her words, v. 12 what wisdom has to offer, v. 13, what she hates, v. 14, more description of her benefits, v. 15-16, her influence, v. 17-21, rewards of seeking her, 22-29 her witness of God's creation, 30-31, her position before God and men, v. 32-36, pros and cons of obedience.

Assignment Nine: read Ch. 9

Assignment Nine: Read Ch. 9

1. Write a short essay comparing and contrasting wisdom and the woman folly. Use specific references to verses in the chapter. Choose one or more of the following topics.

What are their houses like? What does each one offer her guests? What is the end of people who go to each of them?

1-2, *Wisdom has a sturdy house she built herself, plenty of room, food and good things to drink, v. 3, servants, and, v. 4-5, a desire to share what she has for the good of all. v. 6, She offers freedom from foolishness, life, understanding.*

v. 13, the foolish woman also calls out, but she is clamorous, simple, knows nothing. v. 14, also calls from a prominent place to her house, v. 15-16, also seeks to attract the simple, v. 17, but offers what is stolen and secretive, while wisdom is open and provides food from her own efforts. v. 18, the dead and residents of hell are in the foolish woman's house.

Man and Woman

2. Reproving a scorner gets and .
shame, hatred

3. Reproving and instruction a wise man gets what? (2 things).
love, increased learning

4. The fear of the Lord is the beginning of .
wisdom

Assignment Ten: read Ch. 10

Assignment Ten: Read Ch. 10

1. List six benefits or evidences of wisdom, diligence, righteousness, etc. (verses 1-11)
glad father, deliverance from death, safety from famine, riches, gathering in summer, blessings on the just, blessed memory, receive commandments, sure walk, well of life, covering sins.

2. List five punishments for laziness, wickedness, and foolishness.
heaviness to mother, profitless treasures, cast away substance, poverty for stinginess, shameful laziness, violence covering mouth of wicked, name of wicked will rot, prating fool will fall

3. Hatred stirs up , love covers sins.
strifes, all

4. What will happen to the one who is void of understanding?
a rod for his back

Foolishness

5. What is the mouth of the foolish near?
destruction

6. The rich can be protected by their , but poverty leaves the poor unprotected.
wealth

7. The of the righteous tendeth to life: the of the wicked to sin.
labour, fruit

8. Two actions that identify a fool are hatred with lies and uttering .
hiding, slander

9. In the multitude of words there wanteth not .
sin

10. The lips of the righteous many but die for want of wisdom.
feed, fools

11. It is as to a fool to do mischief.
sport

12. As the passeth, so is the wicked no more.
whirlwind

13. The way of the LORD is to the upright: but destruction shall be to the of iniquity.
strength, workers

Assignment Eleven: read Ch. 11

Assignment Eleven: Read Ch. 11

1. List eight kinds of wickedness.
false balance, pride, perverseness, transgressors, naughtiness, hypocrite, void of wisdom, despising neighbor, talebearer, no counsel, cruel, deceitful, pursuing evil, froward heart, no discretion, hoarding ("withholdeth more than is meet"), seeketh mischief, trust in riches, troubles own house

Woman of character

2. List eight demonstrations of righteousness.
just weight, humility ("lowly"), integrity, upright, just, blessing, understanding, uplifting, holding his peace, faithful spirit, trustworthy ("concealeth the matter"), counsel for safety, not going into debt for another ("hating suretyship"), gracious, retaining honor, strong, retaining riches, merciful, sowing righteousness, upright in their way, good desire, generosity ("scattereth, yet increaseth"), sharing, ("the liberal soul shall be made fat"), selling freely, diligently seek good

3. The fruit of the righteous is a of life; and he that winneth souls is .
tree, wise

Assignment Twelve: read Ch. 12

Assignment Twelve: Read Ch. 4

1. Write an essay referencing verses in this chapter contrasting responsibility or diligence with laziness or craftiness.

Some possibilities are: Loving to be taught is contrasted with hating to be corrected (v. 1). One gains knowledge, the other becomes an animal ("brutish"). The Lord favors the efforts of the good but condemns the "devices" of the wicked (v. 2). The good person works and the wicked schemes to avoid work. Wickedness is insecurity, but righteousness is security (v. 3). A woman's virtue gives her husband honor. If she is shameful she causes him suffering. This may even be a reference to giving him a sexually-transmitted disease (v. 4). Righteous people have right thoughts. Wicked counselors are deceitful (v. 5) The wicked attack and injure but the upright save and help (v. 6) Wisdom brings commendations but perversity is scorned (v. 8)

Woman of virtue

2. "The way of a fool is right in his own eyes: but he that hearkeneth unto counsel is wise." (v. 15) Based on what has been taught in Proverbs so far, where does the "counsel" have to come from?
Possible answers include parents' teaching based on God's Word, or from the Lord, through His Word.

3. Find three examples of the benefits of telling the truth. *health-giving, stability (established forever), peace, joy, protection ("no evil happen to"), delighting the Lord, gladness, excellence, respect for effort ("substance ... is precious") life*

4. Find three examples of the punishment for lying.

piercing with a sword, instability ("is but for a moment"), filled with mischief, abomination to the Lord, proclaim foolishness, in another's power ("be under tribute"), weighed down heart, seduced, lazy

Assignment Thirteen: read Ch. 13

Assignment Thirteen: Read Ch. 13

1. Give three advantages gained by good hearing and speech.

receive father's instruction (v. 1), eat what is good (in return for good speech, (v. 2), keep his life (v. 3), be made prosperous ("fat," v. 4), hate lying, be kept safe (v. 6)

Man working

2. "There is that maketh himself , yet hath nothing: there is that maketh himself poor, yet hath great ."
rich, riches.

3. “The light of the righteous : but the lamp of the shall be put out.
rejoiceth, wicked

4. According to verses 10 and 11, pride and vanity produce and loss of .
contention, wealth

Proud man

5. “Hope maketh the heart sick: but when the cometh, it is a tree of life.”
deferred, desire

6. In verses 13-16, all of these words refer to the same thing: “word,” “commandment,” “law,” “good understanding,” “knowledge.” What is it?
The Word of God

7. A wicked messenger falleth into : but a faithful is health.
mischief, ambassador

8. “The desire is sweet to the soul: but it is to fools to depart from evil.” *accomplished, abomination*

9. Write an essay on one of the following topics based on verses 20-25: a) How your parents and your companions

affect your walk b) Righteous provisions in harvest and inheritance

a) choose the company of the wise and wisdom will "rub off" on you. Choose fools and not only will their foolishness influence you, it will destroy you. (v. 20) Keep company with sinners and be pursued by evil. Righteousness will be rewarded. (v. 21) Just as God corrects our sin, our parents can do no less. (v. 24) b) Plan to leave an inheritance to your grandchildren. Expect the wealth of the wicked to pass to the righteous. Righteousness produces satisfaction and contentment. Wickedness produces discontent and craving.

Assignment Fourteen: read Ch. 14

Assignment Fourteen: Read Ch. 14

1. In vv. 1, 3, and 7-9, what are the results of foolish actions?
home destroyed, beating for pride, loss of fellowship, deceitfulness, mocking sin

2. "The heart his own bitterness; and a doth not intermeddle with his joy."
knoweth, stranger

3. In vv. 11-19, The houses, the ways, the inheritances and the positions of both those who do right and those who do wrong are contrasted. List one example of each from each kind of person. The first one is done as an example.

house -- right --- flourish -- wrong -- overthrown)

way -- right -- wrong --

inheritance -- right -- wrong --

position -- right -- wrong --

note that "way" can have four different correct answers) way -- right -- chooses God's way (life) -- wrong -- chooses his way -- death (v. 12)

or right -- personal satisfaction -- wrong -- selfishness (v. 14),

or right -- careful examination of the way -- wrong -- trust without examination (v. 15)

or right -- fearing and departing from evil -- wrong -- raging and overconfidence (v. 16)

inheritance --right -- crowned with knowledge -- wrong -- inherit folly

position -- right -- controlling the gates of the city (leadership) -- wrong -- forced into inferior position and servitude (v. 19)

Hands cupping light

4. Write an essay based on verses 20-24, 31. Discuss the poor, their treatment by others, their contrast to the rich, how foolishness relates to riches, and one way to avoid poverty.

Man's wisdom says to hate and despise the poor but God requires mercy. The friends of the rich may be many but not be genuine (v. 20, 21). Treatment of rich and poor may come from either an evil or a good nature. The reward for good is mercy and truth (v. 22) One way to avoid poverty is to talk less and work more (v. 23). Riches can give honor and power but fools will still be foolish. (v. 24) Cruelty to the poor is an attack on God. Mercy honors God. (v. 31)

5. A witness delivereth souls: but a deceitful witness lies.
true, speaketh

6. The fear of the Lord gives strong , a place of and a of life.
confidence, refuge, fountain

7. To have honor and a continuing kingdom, a king must have .
people

8. Anger and envy damage and .
understanding, life (or health)

9. " exalteth a nation: but is a reproach to any people."
Righteousness, sin

Assignment Fifteen: read Ch. 15

Assignment Fifteen: Read Ch. 15

1. Speaking wisely can turn aside , make right use of , and promote health and .
wrath, knowledge, life

2. "In the house of the righteous is much : but in the of the wicked is trouble. *treasure, revenue*

2. Verse 8 says "The sacrifice of the wicked is an abomination to the Lord." Write an essay researching through the Old Testament passages that teach the sacrifices did not make up for a wrong heart-attitude.

The essay should include Psalm 40:6, Psalm 51:16, Proverbs 21:3, 27, Ecclesiastes 5:1, Hosea 6:6. There may be others. The point to be made is that God wanted a right heart and attitude, humility and obedience, not that the sacrifices were wrong or useless.

Elijah and fiery altar

3. Verses 9-12 make the point that the wicked make their situation worse before God by hating and those who reprove them.
correction, reproof

4. A heart maketh a cheerful countenance: but by sorrow of the heart the spirit is .
merry, broken.

5. Verses 16 and 17 both make the point that great wealth cannot prevent trouble and .
hatred

6. "Without counsel purposes are : but in the of counsellors they are established."
disappointed, multitude

7. "The way of life is to the wise, that he may from hell beneath.
above, above

8. Verse 27 points out that the greedy person's "gifts" (taking bribes) cause trouble not only for him but for
his house

9. Verse 33 warns that before honor comes .
humility

Assignment Sixteen: read Ch. 16

Assignment Sixteen: Read Ch. 16

1. "Commit thy works unto the LORD, and thy shall be established."
thoughts

2. What two things can cause iniquity to be purged?
mercy and truth

Ideal king

3. Write an essay about the ideal king based on vv. 10-15. Do you think this passage justifies the belief European kings had in the "divine right" of kings? Why or why not?

The Scriptures stress over and over that any man can be good or evil, depending on his knowledge of the Scriptures, his obedience to God, and keeping his heart and mind right. Kings of Israel had an especially great responsibility and strict guidelines in the Scriptures for their behavior. The truth is that rather than people accepting the king as a divine judge, the focus of the passage is on the king's responsibility to let God act through him. Verse 14 does not mean that you must be crafty or flattering but that you need to have God's wisdom to make a king understand he has no need to be angry, or to point his anger in the right direction.

4. "The wise in heart shall be called : and the sweetness of the increaseth learning."
prudent, lips

5. Verse 23 teaches that making our hearts wise (by study of the Word) enables us to our mouths and lips, thereby controlling our speech.
teach

6. Verse 27 implies that an ungodly man cannot help but "dig up" or control his ("a burning fire").
evil, lips

7. Verse 33 warns against thinking that decision-making is random chance. Decisions come from
the Lord

Assignment Seventeen: read Ch. 17

Assignment Seventeen: Read Ch. 17

1. Verse 1 contrasts poverty ("a dry morsel") and peace with plenty ("a house full of sacrifices") and .
strife

2. Verse 4 describes a vicious cycle, where the wicked listens to the liar who listens to the tongue.
naughty"

3. Verse 6 states that grandparents can be honored by their grandchildren and children can in their parents.
glory

4. Verse 9 describes a person who "covereth a transgression," that is, does not repeat someone's wrongdoing, because he seeks . However, someone who repeats private sins can be responsible for separating close .
love, friends

5."The beginning of strife is as when one letteth out : therefore leave off before it be meddled with."
water, contention

flooding

6. Wisdom is before him that hath ; but the eyes of a fool are in the of the earth.
understanding, ends

7. According to verse 28, one of the things that allows a fool to at least appear wise is when he
holdeth his peace

Assignment Eighteen: read Ch. 18

Assignment Eighteen: Read Ch. 18

1. Verses 1 and 2 teach that the desire that produces a man is to surround and fill himself ("intermeddleth") with wisdom, but a fool seeks only to himself.
wise, discover

2. Verse 5 warns not to "accept the person of" (give preference or special treatment to) the so that the righteous are in judgment.
wicked, overthrown (note that overthrown means denied justice)

3. Verses 10 and 11 contrast the righteous taking refuge in the and the rich man thinking his wealth is a
Lord, strong city or high wall

Castle

4. Verse 17 says that a man testifying in his own behalf ("first in his own cause") seems but his neighbor may be able to out the facts.
truthful, search

5. Verses 20 and 21 Show that speech has the power to satisfy the body and also the power of .
life and death

6. Verse 23 says that the poor must plead, but the rich can .
answer roughly

Assignment Nineteen: read Ch. 19

Assignment Nineteen: Read Ch. 19

1. Write an essay using verses from Proverbs and explaining some of the truths it teaches about the poor and their relationships to others and God.

Some possibilities include those who are physically poor but spiritually rich, those who trust in riches to protect them as opposed to those who seek protection from the Lord, the wrong attitudes people can have that result in poverty, like laziness, the wrong attitudes people can have toward the poor and how the poor must behave as opposed to the rich. Verses include:11:4, 13:23,14:31, 16:8, 17:5, 19:1, 19:7, 19:17, 21:13, 22:1,22:2, 22:9, 22:16, 22:22-23, 27:7, 28:6, 28:11, 28:27, 29:7, 31:8-9.

Poor child

2. Verses 13 and 14 contrast the behavior of two kinds of wives: and

contentious, prudent

3. Verse 19 teaches that it is useless to try to man of great because he will suffer punishment unless you keep doing it.

deliver, wrath

4. An ungodly witness judgment: and the mouth of the wicked iniquity.

scorneth, devoureth

Assignment Twenty: read Ch. 20

Assignment Twenty: Read Ch. 20

1. According to verse 2, a person who angers a king against his own soul.

sinneth

scales/balances

2. Verses 10 and 23 use the word "Divers," meaning differing, or not consistent, referring to dishonest weights and measures. These verses says these things are an to the Lord.
abomination

3. Verse 19 warns to avoid both a talebearer (gossip) who reveals and a flatterer.
secrets

4. Verse 20 predicts for one who curses his parents.
death

5. Verse 25 says a man will be trapped if he first takes for himself what should be considered and only promises to investigate afterward.
holy

Assignment Twenty-One: read Ch. 21

Assignment Four: Read Ch. 4

1. Verses 1 and 2 point out that God sees into men's hearts, and men only decide what is right in their own .
eyes

2. "The getting of treasures by a lying tongue is a tossed to and fro of them that seek ."
vanity, death

quarrelsome woman

3. Verses 9 and 19 warn that having no house at all is better than living with a and woman.
brawling, angry

4. Verses 25 and 26 warn against laziness, that it can and results in greed rather than being generous.
kill, coveting

Assignment Twenty-two: Read Ch. 22

Assignment Twenty-two: Read Ch. 22

1. Verses 1, 2 and 4 discuss riches. What is one thing to be chosen over riches?What do the rich and poor have in common? What can result in getting riches, honor and life?
good name or loving favor, the Lord as Maker, humility, the fear of the Lord

2. Verses 3 and 5 contrast the paths of the self-controlled ("prudent," "he that keepeth his soul") and the simple or froward. The former "forseeth the evil" and but the latter

finds punishment, .
hideth himself, thorns and snares

3. Verse 10 promises a cure for contention and strife, if you are willing to .
cast out the scorner

Scorner

4. In verse 14, one of the punishments God promises to those who make themselves hateful to Him is that they will be helpless in the power of a .
strange woman

5. "Foolishness is in the heart of a child; but the rod of correction shall it far from him."
bound, drive

6. Verses 17-21 promise that applying your heart to the knowledge of God will result in (list three things)
pleasantness, wise words on your lips, trust in the Lord, certainty of truth, answer with words of truth those who ask

7. Verses 22 and 23 promise that those who rob the poor will have their souls by the Lord.
spoiled

Assignment Twenty-Three: read Ch. 23

Assignment Twenty-three: Read Ch. 23

1. Verses 1-8 deal with riches, rulers, "dainties," and flattery. Write an essay on God's perspective about the problems of seeking riches for their own sake bring, as well as trying to form relationships with the ungodly for personal advancement.

This passage admonishes us not to be deceived and think that riches will satisfy us or make us happy. We must not allow our appetites to control us. Our reason wants us to strive to be rich. Riches do not endure. Often the rich are evil, not to be trusted, and their food is not good for us. Their whole plan is to lull "guests" into false security and get power over them. What we eat may make us sick, physically and spiritually, and flattery makes us liars. We become corrupted, weak, and easy prey for the wicked.

2. Verses 10 and 11 warn us that we cannot remove old , thinking that we have the power to cheat the .we must never forget that we are responsible to the great , who will judge us.
boundaries, fatherless, Redeemer

3. Verses 13 and 14 admonish us not to be afraid to a child, knowing that it will not cause his death, but rather

his soul from Hell.
correct (or beat), deliver

4. Verses 17 and 18 warn not to sinners, but to be in the fear of the Lord, so that our will not be cut off in the end.
envy, expectation

5. Verse 20, 21, and 29-35 warn of the dangers of drunkenness and those given to excess. List five things it can lead to.
Some possibilities are riotousness, poverty, laziness, woe, sorrow, contentions, babbling, wounds without cause, red eyes, poisoning, delusions, perverse speech, numbness, recklessness, addiction

drunken woman

6. The father of the righteous shall greatly and the mother of a son shall rejoice.
rejoice, wise

7. A prostitute is like a and like a wild animal stalking prey. She increases .
pit, transgressors

Assignment Twenty-Four: read Ch. 24

Assignment Twenty-four: Read Ch. 24

1. Do not to envy evil men who study but seek wisdom and understanding, to build and to .
destruction, establish

2. Verses 10-12 warn of the consequences of pretending to be ignorant of other people's danger. Write an essay describing how this applies to those who know the Word of God and fail to warn people of the consequences of sin.

Indifferent woman

Verse 10 describes weakness in the face of opposition to truth or persecution. Verse 11 tells us we have power in our knowledge of the Scriptures to deliver the lost, or even believers who might be threatened for their faith. Verse 12 says we cannot claim we didn't know the lost or the persecuted were in danger, because God knows the truth, and our hearts.

3. Verses 15 and 16 say that though a just man may fall, he will but the wicked, especially those who lay in wait against the will fall into mischief.
rise up again, righteous

4. List three things we are not to do concerning evil men or enemies.
rejoice at their fall, be glad at their stumbling, fret because of them, envy them

5. In verses 23-26, Those who call the righteous will be cursed and abhorred, but those who them cause delight and receive blessing.
wicked, rebuke

6. Verses 30-34 give a lesson from studying the farm of a lazy man. List three things that happen because of laziness.
overgrown with thorns and nettles, wall broken down, oversleeping, poverty, "stolen" productivity

Assignment Twenty-five: read Ch. 25

Assignment Twenty-five: Read Ch. 25

1. Verses 2-7 talk about kings. Write an essay about how kings should behave and how we should behave toward them.

God does not always openly tell us all things, but a king should want to study and learn as much as he can. A king's heart should not be easy for people to understand and influence. As refining purifies silver so removing wicked people from a kingdom refines the king. Be humble around a king, so that he can give you a high position instead of having to put you down lower because someone more worthy arrives.

2. Verses 8-10 warn against quarreling with your neighbor publicly. List three things you should do or not do.
resolve your complaint with him, keep it confidential, avoid being embarrassed in public, don't get a reputation as a quarreler.

3. Verses 11-13 praise the good use of words. They are like an ornament of fine , and they the soul.
gold, refresh

4. Verse 18 compares a man that about his neighbors to destructive tools and weapons.
lies

5. Find the parallel New Testament use of verses 21-22.
Romans 12:20

6. Verse 26 warns that the should not fall before the wicked, physically or spiritually.
righteous

Beehive

7. Verses 16 and 27 warn that eating too much honey is like seeking your own .
glory

8. Verse 28 compares lack of self-control to a city without
.
walls

Assignment Twenty-Six: read Ch. 26

Assignment Twenty-six: Read Ch. 26

1. Based on verses 1-12, discuss the fool and foolish behavior.

Don't waste honor on a fool, don't pay attention to curses, punish foolishness in a person just as you would in an animal, don't answer foolishness with more foolishness, don't let a fool think he is right if he isn't, don't trust a fool with important work, don't expect a fool to make sense and beware that his foolishness can be harmful, know that God punishes fools as He does those who disobey Him, expect a fool to repeat his folly, no matter how disgusting, and even a fool is better off than a man who is conceited.

Lazy man

2. List three practices of a lazy man from verses 13-16. *claiming it's dangerous to go outside, tossing in bed all day, too lazy to eat what's in front of him (or possibly fearful it will be taken away), self-centered and self-justifying.*

3. From verses 18-28, list three kinds of deceptions and three kinds of consequences or dangers from them.

Deceptions: jokes ("am I not in sport?"), talebearer (gossip), constantly arguing (contentious, kindling strife), lying to destroy another's reputation (disembleth), pretending to "speak fair," plotting destruction for another (digging a pit), lying to cause pain ("hateth those afflicted by it"), flattering mouth.

Consequences: firebrands, arrows, death, (also the joker thought to be a madman), strife ends when the gossiping ceases, making a bad situation worse, causing deep emotional wounds, never to be trusted, becoming full of abominations, deceptive appearance of prosperity, obsession with deceiving and hating, disgraceful exposure to the public, caught in the trap set for others, afflicting and ruining others.

Assignment Twenty-Seven: read Ch. 27

Assignment Twenty-seven: Read Ch. 27

1. You should not boast about tomorrow for what two reasons?

a. you don't know what will happen tomorrow; b. better to let others praise you

Boasting man

2. Write an essay on good and harmful relationships based on verses 3-21.

Living around someone who is always angry is like trying to carry heavy loads -- exhausting and weakening. Envy can be worse than outright anger. Someone who corrects your faults openly is better than someone who claims to love you in private. A friend might hurt your feelings by telling you when you are wrong, but an enemy will pretend to support you while knowing you will fail. Hunger makes us appreciate what we have. Men sometimes wander with no good purpose from the place where they belong. Good friendship and counsel is as welcome as a pleasant scent. Respect and take advantage of friendship. Don't prefer family when friends are nearer. Make your parents proud of you and be trustworthy even if someone slanders you. Be wise enough to avoid evil, unlike people who dive in and suffer consequences. Don't trust people who cosign for someone of unknown or bad character. Don't show off your virtue by loud blessings and make people despise you. Don't be a woman who is known for arguing, and don't think you can ignore one. Make a friend better, like a whetstone sharpens a tool, and look for friends who "sharpen" you. Do a good job for your employer and he will honor you. You can demonstrate trustworthiness and see it in others. You will never get everything you want, and you might find destruction. A man can be encouraged to improve by praise.

3. Verses 22-27 show the contrast between being unable to the foolishness out of a fool with a mortar and pestle and the rewards for those who are diligent: Not necessarily riches or a kingdom, but the of your household.
grind, food

Assignment Twenty-Eight: read Ch. 28

Assignment Twenty-eight: Read Ch. 28

1. "The wicked flee when no man but the righteous are as a lion.
pursueth, bold

Lion

2. Write an essay on the use and abuse of the laws of government and commerce as described in verses 2-12.

Wicked lands have many rulers because with evil comes constant fickleness, treachery, jealousy, assassinations, and plots to overthrow one ruler in favor of another. A good ruler will by knowledge and understanding be able to preserve a stable rule. Poor oppressing poor destroys any hope that anyone will be prosperous. Forsaking law results in supporting wickedness. Keeping the law will make you want to fight evil. Those who are evil have no appreciation for justice. The Lord gives understanding in matters of law. It is better to be poor and do right than to be rich and lawless. Rioters disgrace their families. The generous will get control of wealth gained by injustice. God hates hypocritical prayers from people who scorn law. Causing the righteous to go astray can result in being caught in one's own trap. The poor can have discernment to shame the self-important rich. The righteous share the glorious results of their success but people hide from wicked rulers.

3. "He that covereth his shall not prosper: but whoso confesseth and them shall have mercy." *sins, forsaketh*

4. Verses 15 and 16 compare wicked rulers who are great to those who hate .
oppressors, coveteousness

5. "He that rebuketh a man afterwards shall find more than he that flattereth with the tongue."
favor

6. Verse 26 warns against trusting your own and promises to those who walk wisely.
heart, deliverance

Assignment Twenty-nine: read Ch. 29

Assignment Twenty-nine: Read Ch. 29

1. "He, that being often reproved , his neck, shall suddenly be destroyed, and that without ."
hardeneth, remedy

stubborn man

2. Verse 3 contrasts wisdom making a father with sexual license, which destroys the family's .
rejoice, substance

3. Verse 8 says that a trap awaits the city run by the but wise men can turn away .
scornful, wrath

4. "When the are multiplied, transgression increaseth: but the righteous shall see their ."
wicked, fall

5. If you partner with a thief, you hate your own . You don't even mind when you hear
soul, cursing

6. When it comes to the just man and the unjust man, the feeling is mutual. Both consider the other to be an .
abomination

Assignment Thirty: read Ch. 30

Assignment Thirty: Read Ch. 30

1. This verse introduces a different author from the one who wrote most of Proverbs. His name is .
Agur

2. Verses 2-6 seem to echo the writing of what other book of the Bible where a man was humbled when confronted by the reality of God's holiness and His control over nature? Here is an example: "Who is this that darkeneth counsel by words without knowledge? Gird up now thy loins like a man; for I will demand of thee, and answer thou me. Where wast thou when I laid the foundations of the earth? declare, if thou hast understanding." *Job*

Earth

3. Verses 7-9 present a very unusual request to be made as a matter of life and death. Briefly summarize this petition.

Answers will vary but should include taking away empty, meaningless things and falsehoods, preventing too much either of plenty or want, just enough food for comfort, so that he will not forget to honor God for his provision, nor will he be tempted to steal and bring disgrace to God's name.

4. List four characteristics of the "Generation" of evildoers described in verses 11-14.
curse, and refuse to bless, parents, pure in own eyes, filthy, proud, teeth and jaws like swords, devouring the poor and needy

5. Name two of the four things that are never satisfied.
grave, barren womb, dry earth, fire

6. Choose either the "four things too wonderful to know (understand)," or the "four things that disquiet the earth," and name three of them.

1st set: eagle in the air, serpent upon a rock, ship in the midst of the sea; man with a maid.

2nd set: servant when he reigneth; fool when he is filled with meat, odious woman when married, handmaid heir to mistress.

7. Name two of the four little but wise things and include the description.
conies feeble folk, homes in rocks, locusts, no king, go by bands, spider in king's palaces.

Assignment Thirty-one: read Ch. 31

Assignment Thirty-one: Read Ch. 31

1. Verse one introduces another author. What is his name?
King Lemuel

2. The king's mother warns him against what two things?
women who destroy kings and strong drink

3. Strong drink will make kings forget and is only to be given to those who are .
the law, perishing, or have heavy hearts, poverty, or misery

4. Two things a king should do is to speak for those who and plead the cause of the poor and .
can't speak for themselves ("dumb"), needy

virtuous woman

5. List eight characteristics of the virtuous woman.

price above rubies, husband's heart trusts her, he has no need for spoil, do husband good, not evil, all her life, works willingly, brings food from afar, rises at night to feed household and servants, good business sense, works at growing good crops, keeps herself strong, keeps busy day and night making things to share with the poor, clothe her family and adorn herself. She helps her husband to a good reputation, produces products for sale, is known for strength, honor and joyful prospects, is wise and kind, manages her house and herself well, is blessed and praised by husband and children, excellent among daughters, fearing the Lord, not concerned about shallow approval or beauty, rewarded and praised by those in authority.

Sculptures from the Twelve Prophets of Aleijandino 1800–1805

Congonlias do Campo, forecourt of the Sanctuario do Bom Jesus de Matosinhos.
Photos by -- Eric Gaba (Daniel and Isaiah) and Luis Rizo (Ezekiel) -- Wikimedia Commons

Study Guide for the Background to the Major Prophets

"Study to shew thyself approved unto God, a workman that needeth not to be ashamed, rightly dividing the word of truth." 2 Timothy 2:15

https://www.youtube.com/@ffvp5657

These lessons are designed to give a setting, background and introduction to the time period we know as the Major Prophets. The dates given follow *The Bible Knowledge Commentary*, John F. Walvoord and Roy B. Zuck.

Fall of Samaria by William Brassey Hole

The first major prophet is Isaiah, though he wrote from Jerusalem during the Assyrian invasion which saw the fall of Samaria. With the fall of Samaria, the Northern Kingdom went into captivity. Isaiah prophesied for at least 58 years, beginning in 739 BC, though he could have started earlier and ministered longer. Isaiah is almost one hundred years earlier than the other three Major Prophets.

Jeremiah by Rembrant Wikimedia Commons

The first of these three is Jeremiah. Jeremiah was a priest who began prophesying during the reign of Josiah. Josiah reigned for thirty-one years, from 640 BC to 609 BC. Jeremiah prophesied for at least forty-five years, from 627 BC until around 582 BC. He prophesied during the reigns of all the kings up to the exile. He saw the fall of Jerusalem in 586 BC.

The next major prophet, in the order of our English Bible, would be Ezekiel. Ezekiel was, like Jeremiah, a priest. He began his ministry when he was thirty years old in the 5th year of King Jehoiachin's captivity. He went into exile the second time Nebuchadnezzar came against Jerusalem in 597 BC, the 8th year of Nebuchadnezzar. He was carried away with his family to live in Babylon. He had his own home in Babylon on the Chebar River, which today we call the royal canal of Nebuchadnezzar.

Ezekiel by John Singer Sargent

Daniel was the third (or fourth, if we count Isaiah) major prophet, though he never exercised what we think of today as the office of prophet. He was a government administrator. He was carried away in 605 BC as a child the first time Babylonian army led by the not yet king Nebuchadnezzar came against Jerusalem. Though Nebuchadnezzer led the Babylonian armies, his father Nebopolassar, was still alive and still had the title king.

We know that Daniel had to be quite young at this time because he lived at least until the first year of Cyrus, king of Persia, 539 BC. The events recorded in the book of Daniel begin in the middle of Jeremiah's ministry and more than a decade before the beginning of Ezekiel's ministry.

Daniel's Answer to the King by Briton Riviere Public Domain

I am unaware of anyone who really loves to study dates, but dates and chronology are the backbone of history. The Exodus of the Children of Israel out of Egypt occurred in 1446 BC. It is the foundation for all other dating throughout the Old Testament. We know this because I Kings 6:1 says that "480 years after the Children of Israel had left Egypt in the fourth year of Solomon's reign, in the second month, the month of Zif, they began building the temple." Solomon's temple establishes a very clear date for us.

In a very quick overview, after the Children of Israel left Egypt they went to Mount Sinai, then to Kadesh-barnea where they were condemned to wander for forty years.

They entered the land of promise and the time period of the judges was around three hundred fifty to four hundred years. Then we see the last judge and the founder of the school of the prophets, Samuel. The exact beginning and ending of the period of the judges are difficult to date.

Joshua led the Children of Israel across the Jordan River into the Promised Land about 1405 BC. The division of the land by Joshua was probably ten years later, about 1395 BC. The ending of the period of the Judges is even more difficult to date. Samuel and Samson were almost certainly contemporaries. David's reign overlapped Saul's in the beginning and Solomon's at the end, making exact dating of the beginning of Saul's reign difficult. If you are interested in working these dates out, I recommend *The Mysterious Numbers of the Hebrew Kings* by Edwin R. Thiele.

The campaigns which Joshua led did not take place overnight. In fact, some people think that they might have taken place over twenty years. Most conservatives think that they took about five. After the campaign was finished, Eleazar was still the high priest. Eleazar was probably alive at Kadesh-barnea but under twenty years old, therefore he was allowed to enter the land. This would have made Eleazar between forty-one and fifty-nine when the Children of Israel crossed the Jordan River into the promised land under Joshua. Phinehas, Eleazar's son and Aaron's grandson was born during the wilderness wanderings.

Baal image found in Ugarit from the Louvre Wikimedia Commons Photographer Marie Lan Nguyen

While the Children of Israel were waiting to cross the Jordan River, the sin of Baal-Peor occurred, where Phinehas drove a spear through both an Israelite leader and a Moabite woman. So Phinehas was old enough to wield a spear while Moses was still alive. Phinehas was the High Priest according to the book of Judges during the horrible incidents in Judges 17. This was the near-extinction of the tribe of Benjamin. It also gives us a time frame for the book of Judges.

Public domain image of Phinehas

Since Phinehas was the High Priest, those events happened, not during Joshua's lifetime, but near the beginning of the period of the Judges. The people who participated in the conquest of Canaan as young men were now the elders. The people who were rebelling against the Lord had never seen the conquest of Canaan.

The next to the last major judge mentioned in the book of Judges before Samuel was Jephthah. In Judges 11, he sent messengers unto the king of the children of Ammon when the children of Ammon attacked Gilead. The king of the children of Ammon claimed that the children of Israel had taken away their land. Jephthah responded to the children of Ammon that the children of Israel had occupied Heshbon, Aroer and the surrounding settlements all along the Arnon River for three hundred years already.

The Arnon is the river which flows from East to West into the Jordan River, through what we think of today as the country of Jordan. Even if Jephthah was using round numbers, that is, approximating, he sent those messengers about eleven hundred BC or about one hundred thirty years before Solomon began building the temple.

Samuel was the last of the judges. But he was also the first of the prophets. He anointed Saul and began the united monarchy. Samuel's children had displeased both the children of Israel and the Lord by their sin. So God chose Saul, but Saul turned away from the Lord. The Amalekites which Saul defeated lived in a city. They were not, as all secular historians teach, a little group of Bedouins.

Remember Balaam's prophecy where he said they were the first among the nations? First among the nations is not a group of Bedouins. When Saul defeated them he propelled Israel to the status of a great world power.

David took them further with the defeat of the Philistines and Solomon in all of his splendor made Israel the greatest nation on earth. After the wealth and greatness of Solomon, Rehoboam chose to ignore the Lord even further. His father Solomon had turned from the Lord and as Solomon grew older he departed more and more from following the Lord.

Scale model of the temple in Jerusalem

Rehoboam continued on this downward path. Rehoboam caused the rebellion of the Northern tribes and we see the divided kingdom. The Northern kingdom became very powerful in its own right. In fact, during the reign of Jeroboam II, an honest observer might have had difficulty trying to determine whether this nation of Israel or the Assyrians would be the next world power. However, by rebelling further against the Lord, the Northern Kingdom went into captivity to the Assyrians in 722 BC.

The Southern Kingdom at that time had Hezekiah as king. The Assyrians captured every city in the Southern Kingdom except Jerusalem. All the rest of the lands were lost to the invading armies of Assyria. Isaiah the prophet prophesied during this time. Hezekiah had a son, named Manasseh, who followed his father to the throne and became the most wicked king of either Israel or Judah. This eventually led to the destruction of Judah, the Southern Kingdom. They finally went into captivity to the Babylonians when Jerusalem fell in 586 BC. This is the period of the Major Prophets.

This next section deals with the anti-supernatural bias which you will find reading virtually anybody who writes about the Old Testament today. This anti-supernatural bias demands that historical artifacts, objects, testimony and even modern scholarship place things out of order based on the way the evidence presents itself. We will take a very quick look at a few areas where this anti-supernatural bias is most obvious to the public.

The first evidence of ant-supernatural bias is making uniformitarian assumptions. Sometimes called "the present is the key to the past," it is a religious belief that the past can be analyzed in terms of present processes. It is the rigid belief that worldwide catastrophes have not occurred in the historic past. They believe that any and all worldwide catastrophes occurred before the arrival of civilization.

They believe in local catastrophes such as the eruption of Mount Vesuvius, tsunamis or earthquakes. But Plato's description of the destruction of the entire continent of Atlantis in one night is considered impossible. The sun standing still for Joshua or going backwards for Hezekiah are dismissed out of hand. A world-wide flood which destroyed all life on earth as a judgment on sin is viciously attacked.

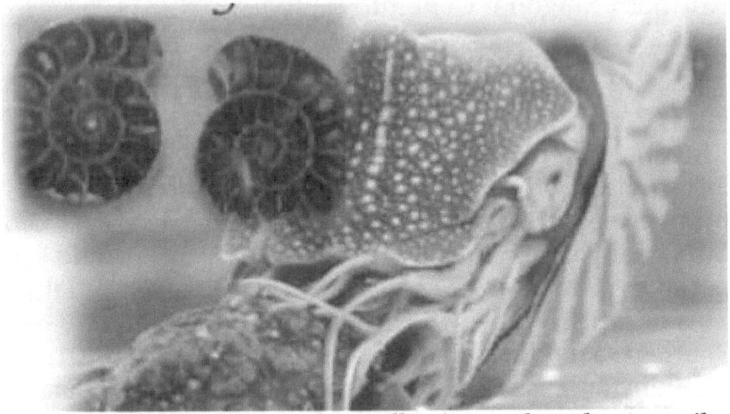

Ammonite fossils from author collection and modern nautilus

Second, evidence contrary to an anti-supernatural bias is censored. One example is the top of Mount Everest. When Sir Edmund Hillary climbed Mt. Everest in 1953, one of his motives was to find the marine fossils near the top which he had heard about. He found an enormous number of intact marine fossils called ammonites in a layer near the top. This proves that the Himalayan mountains were formed in a sudden, catastrophic event. In order for the Ammonites to remain intact, they had to be put in place while they were still moist. Only if the layer around them was still mud, would they be preserved intact. However, since water weighs approximately eight pounds per gallon, it could not remain moist for a long, slow upthrust.

Third is massive misinformation. Ten different serious professional geologists can examine the exact same strata and they will usually come up with ten different dates. Yet museums and parks all across the world have identified fossils, geologic formations and historical artifacts with specific dates. Even dating the founding of Carthage, a known city with abundant written records, is difficult.

Another example of how history is being distorted today is this idea that neolithic man was a simple stone age man, that he was a cave dweller. Well, today people live in caves. Sometimes for shelter, sometimes just for a party but for whatever reason there is no indication that the culture of people who lived in caves was vastly inferior to the culture today. There is not even any indication that most of the people who were living on earth were living in caves at that time. They might have been temporary shelters as people were going about hunting. They might have been shelters for people who were sailing or exploring. We do not know the purpose. But we do know that if we accept this evolutionary dogma of moving from the simpler to the complex that we will never understand what we are looking at when we examine ancient history.

As far as our studies in the Book of Daniel, the next major issue is accuracy. Daniel's prophecies are so accurate and so detailed that the secular humanists with an anti-supernatural bias who believe that there is no such thing as prophetic revelation, demand a late date for Daniel. These are not prophecies, according to them. These "so-called prophecies," (that is what they say, had to be written after the fact.

Major Prophets Background Questions

Major Prophets Background Questions

1. Who was the first major prophet, who wrote during the reign of Hezekiah in Jerusalem and the fall of Samaria to the Assyrians? *Isaiah*

2. About how many years passed before the other three major prophets wrote?*100*

3. Who are the other three major prophets? *Jeremiah, Ezekiel, Daniel*

4. Of these three, which one is the oldest? *Jeremiah*

5. Generally speaking, match each of these three prophets with the location where he ministered and who he ministered to. *Jeremiah-Jerusalem, Judah; he ministered to thoseJews left behind: Ezekiel-in his own house by the Chebar River (the Grand Canal) in Babylon; he ministered to the Jews taken into exile: Daniel-the palace of Nebuchadnezzar in Babylon; he ministered to the royal staff*

6. What is the date (in the Gregorian Calendar) for the fall of Jerusalem to the Babylonians? *586 BC*

7. What is the date for the Exodus of the Children of Israel from Egypt? *1446 BC*

8. What verse in the Bible gives us the date of the Exodus? *I Kings 6:1*

9. What does it say? *Solomon began the temple 480 years after the Exodus*

10. Who was Phinehas? *grandson of Aaron, son of Eleazar high priest after his father*

11. What two events is Phinehas connected with which help us establish a chronology? *Speared leading Israelite man and leading Moabite woman. Stop plague, Baal-Peor before Israel crossed Jordan. Moses was still alive.*

When old, high priest, Judges 17. Children of Israel punished sin of Benjamin.

12. Who was the next to the last major judge who sent a message to the king of Ammon and told how long the Gileadites had been in the land?
Jephthah

13. How long did he say that the children of Israel had been in the land?
300 years

14. Who was the last judge and the first of the prophets?
Samuel

15. What other judge was probably still alive when he was a little boy?
Samson

16. Who did he anoint king over all Israel?
Saul and David

17. Who did Saul defeat, which put Israel on the path to become a great world power?
Amalak (Amalakites)

18. David's defeat of what nation greatly advanced Israel's military might?
Philistines

19. What king took Israel to the position of a world power?
Solomon

20. Who was the last king of the united monarchy?
Rehoboam

21. Militarily, who was the strongest king of the northern kingdom?
Jeroboam II

22. With what other rising power was Israel competing?
Assyria

23. Who destroyed the Northern Kingdom?
Assyria

24. What was the capital of the Northern Kingdom?
Samaria

25. What year did the Northern Kingdom go into captivity?
722 BC

26. What did Hezekiah lose in the Assyrians invasion?
everything except Jerusalem

27. Hezekiah's son, wicker than any king of Israel or Judah, was named what?
Manasseh

28. What year did Jerusalem fall?
586 BC

29. To what kingdom and king did Jerusalem fall?
Babylon, Nebuchadnezzar

30. What bias makes it difficult to read history books?
Anti-supernatural

31. List three examples of this bias.
uniformitarian assumptions, censorship of honest historical research, massive misinformation

32. Were there neolithic men?
Yes, but there is no evidence that they were any different from modern men.

33. Daniel's prophecies were extremely accurate. How do unbelievers deal with Daniel?
They claim that Daniel was written after the events about which he prophesied.

Optional Essays and Research Projects

1. Map the positions of Israel and its enemies at different periods. For example: a) First encounters, b) Israel dominating, c) Israel declining/defeated

2. Research and write about the direct relationships of the Major Prophets with the kings they served under. (Remember that some served under several kings).

3. Research to write about times when men temporarily lived in caves and left evidences that archaeologists could misinterpret as true habitation. Examples would be after natural disasters, during migrations, or to escape invaders.

4. Research Daniel's prophecies and when they were fulfilled.

Jonah

The Slow of Heart

Bible Study Series Part Two

"Oh, fools, and slow of heart, to believe all that the prophets have spoken: ought not Christ have suffered these things and to enter into His glory? and beginning at Moses and all the prophets he expounded unto them in all the scriptures the things concerning Himself."

With Commentary by the Anything Box Puppets

Jonah: The Slow of Heart Bible Story Series, Part Two

"Oh, fools, and slow of heart, to believe all that the prophets have spoken: ought not Christ have suffered these things and to enter into His glory? and beginning at Moses and all the prophets he expounded unto them in all the scriptures the things concerning Himself."

Luke 24:25-26

With Commentary by the Anything Box Puppets

This version of Jonah is designed to give a complete, accurate account of the biblical narrative and as a study guide for younger readers. It is a companion to a set of videos available free on YouTube.

https://www.youtube.com/@ffvp5657

Prologue –On the Road to Emmaus

Two men walked along the dusty road to Emmaus.

"We did not understand," one said. "He knew He was going to die. He told us it would happen, remember?"

"There were so many things we did not understand, Thaddeus," said his friend, whose name was Cleopas, "about the kingdom, about how we should live -- about heaven."

"Hello, friends. May I join you? What are you talking about?"

The two men turned in surprise as a stranger came up behind them. It was he who had spoken.

"Have you heard nothing about all that has happened in Jerusalem these past few days?" Cleopas asked.

"Tell me," the stranger said.

"Jesus of Nazareth, the one who was such a mighty prophet, has been killed," Thaddeus explained. "Our rulers and priests turned him over to the Romans and they crucified him."

"That was three days ago," Cleopas told the stranger. "But some of our friends who followed him have told us that they have seen him alive."

“Foolish fellows,” the stranger said, shaking his head. “These things had to happen to Jesus-- His suffering was foretold by the prophets. From the time of Moses -- all through the scriptures it is told. Remember Jonah?”

“Jonah? What about Jonah?” Cleopas asked.

“Wait! Jonah!” cried Thaddeus. “ I remember a time when the Pharisees were pestering Him ... ‘It is only by Beelzebub, the prince of demons, that this fellow drives out demons.’“

“‘Teacher, we want to see a miraculous sign from You,’“ mocked Cleopas. “I remember that too.”

“They were trying to get Him to do more miracles just so they could get Him into trouble,” Thaddeus said sadly. “What has Jonah got to do with it?” Cleopas asked the stranger.

The stranger replied, “The Lord said, ‘A wicked and adulterous generation asks for a miraculous sign. But none will be given it except the sign of the prophet Jonah.’“

“Jonah ... Jonah ... I do seem to remember something like that ... What was it He said?” Thaddeus asked.

“‘As Jonah was three days and three nights in the belly of a huge fish,” said the stranger, “‘so the Son of Man will be three days and three nights in the heart of the Earth.’“

“I suppose being in the heart of the Earth must mean His death. But He will be there longer than three days!” Cleopas said.

“Listen to the story of Jonah. I’ll tell it as we walk,” the stranger suggested. “It began with ... the Word of the Lord ...

Chapter One – Nineveh or Tarshish?

God said to Jonah, "Arise, Jonah, son of Amittai. Go to the great city of Nineveh, and preach against it, because its wickedness has come up before me."

Jonah was afraid. "Nineveh? How can I go there? They're our enemies. They might kill me. If I preached to them they might - Repent! They deserve to be punished for their sins. Lord, You didn't say Nineveh, did you?"

All the while Jonah hurried through his washing and breakfast, then began packing his things.

"I must have been mistaken. Maybe God said, 'Get as far away from Nineveh as you can.' Yes! He's finally going to punish them for their wickedness."

Jonah got out a map. "I'll go to Tarshish -- That's as far in the opposite direction as I can go. I'll head for the port of Joppa right away!"

Chapter Two –The Port of Joppa

Later Jonah stood on a dock at the port of Joppa. A ship captain stood nearby, shouting orders to his crew as they loaded a ship called the Black Swan.

"Get moving, you lazy sons of jackals. Baal won't help you if we miss the tide! Hoist that on deck. Heave those bales into the hold. Get some life into you!"

Jonah picked up his heavy bag and followed the captain, trying to get his attention. "Excuse me. Ahem! I "

The captain turned and ran into Jonah. His bag fell to the ground, tripping a sailor who fell into another sailor, until the captain, Jonah, and all the sailors lay in a heap on the dock.

The captain roared, "Stop following me around! Can't you see we're trying to load this ship? The Black Swan sails for Tarshish with the tide!"

Jonah nodded eagerly. "I know! I want to sail with you. I've got to get to Tarshish right away!" He held out a bag of coins.

The captain growled, "This is a cargo ship. The *Bounding Hind* over there -- She's a passenger ship. Leaves in the morning."

"I can't wait that long!" cried Jonah. "I've got to go now!"

"Why? Are you running away from something?" The captain snatched the bag and jingled it to see how many coins it held.

"I just need to go right away, that's all."

"All right, then, my fat little passenger," grinned the captain, jingling the coins again and putting the bag inside his shirt. "I'll take you to Tarshish." He turned to go back to work. Then he faced Jonah again. "If you cause me trouble I'll toss you in the sea. Now get below and stay out of my way."

"Oh, yes! Oh, yes! I won't be any trouble!" Jonah followed some sailors aboard ship as the captain continued to work. The sailors stopped on deck after they made sure the captain was not watching.

"What are you so scared of?" asked the first sailor. "Go on! Stow your stuff."

"We might need help later," laughed the second sailor, "but I doubt a little butterball like you can do much good."

"Anyway, this should be an easy voyage," said the first sailor.

"Get back to work!" snarled the captain.

A sailor shoved Jonah down into hold, from bright sunlight into pitch darkness.

Chapter Three -- The Storm

The voyage had barely begun when a huge storm broke. Cracks of thunder grew louder and more fierce. Thunder, wind, crashing waves, creaking wood, and shouting filled the air.

Lightning flashed as the ship rolled and heaved. The captain and sailors struggled with ropes, sails and cargo.

"I've never seen a storm like this!" screamed a sailor.

"The ship's going to break up!" another moaned.

"Throw the cargo overboard!" ordered the captain. "All of it! We've got to lighten the ship."

"Those merchants will squawk about losing their goods!" said a sailor.

"I hope we'll be alive to hear them complain!" another sailor answered.

"Every man pray to your gods!" said the captain. "Someone must save us or we'll all die!"

"Poseidon! God of the sea! Save us from this storm!"

"Help us, Molech!" Sailors fell on their knees, raised their hands to sky, and pulled out lucky charms and idols.

They dumped cargo overboard and continued to struggle with the ship.

“Where’s that passenger we brought aboard?” demanded the captain.

“I haven’t seen him since we sailed,” a sailor answered. “He must still be below.”

The captain hurried down into the hold. Jonah lay asleep, snoring. The captain shook Jonah and pulled off his covers.

“Sleeping?” the Captain said. “In this storm? Get up and pray to your God!

The ship is breaking up! Maybe He will save us.”

The captain and Jonah struggled up on deck. The captain returned to his duties. Jonah moved aside and knelt on the deck.

Sailors nearby cast lots.

“Someone must be the cause of this storm. Let’s cast lots to find out who it is.”

“It’s him!” shouted a sailor, pointing at Jonah. All the crew and the captain gathered around Jonah. He got up nervously.

The captain demanded, “Who are you? Where do you come from?”

“I’m a Hebrew,” Jonah told them. “The true God, Who made the sea and dry land, told me to go preach in Nineveh, and I ran for Tarshish instead!”

“How can we make the sea calm?” cried a sailor.

“Throw me into the sea, and it will become calm. I know it’s my fault this storm came.”

“We can’t just drown him,” exclaimed a sailor.

“We’ll try to bring the ship to land,” said the captain.

The crew rowed hard but the ship was about to break up. "It's no use," the captain said. "We'll have to do what the prophet says. Oh, Lord God, do not blame us for this man's death. You have done what You pleased."

The sailors picked up Jonah and threw him overboard. The storm immediately ended.

The sailors and the captain fell on their knees.

"What a mighty God!" said the captain.

"He is the true God!" "We will serve Him from now on."

Jonah heard these cries from the ship's crew as he bobbed away from the ship. Then he felt a huge rush of water beneath him. He looked down and saw a gigantic dark shape come up beneath him in the water. A huge fish opened its great mouth and Jonah felt himself going down, down, down....

Chapter Four – Inside the Great Fish

Jonah realized he had been swallowed by the great fish. He got up on his hands and knees and looked around. Beneath and all around him was soft, sticky red-gray wetness. Gurgling, foamy liquid gushed around him.

Jonah began to pray. "In my distress I called to the Lord, and He answered me." A sucking sound like a whirlpool frightened him. He felt himself going down again, swirling around and around. He struggled to stay out of the deep, black hole.

"From the depths of the grave I called for help, and You listened to my cry."

Jonah realized he had been shouting over all the noise. But suddenly he heard soft voices, faraway-sounding, chanting and singing parts of the worship service in the temple at Jerusalem. In his mind he saw the beautiful house of God, golden, misty, like a dream. He reached toward it.

"I will look again toward Your holy temple," Jonah sighed.

Then Jonah heard violent sea sounds, waves, and wind. He remembered the sounds from the ship to Tarshish -- ropes snapping -- thunder like an earthquake. Seaweed from the great fish's belly swirled around and wrapped him up head to foot.

"The engulfing waters threatened me, the deep surrounded me; the seaweed was wrapped around my head. To the roots of the mountains I sank down; the earth beneath barred me forever."

Then once again the sounds of the service in the temple of the Lord grew. The storms and rushing water quieted. Jonah looked up from the deep darkness and saw light growing around him. Sparkling foam rushed past as he broke the surface of the water into sunshine. Far in the distance he saw the shining temple on a hillside.

"But You brought my life up from the pit, O Lord my God. When my life was ebbing away, I remembered You, Lord, and my prayer rose to You, to Your holy temple."

Jonah saw the scene change suddenly to a pagan temple with people worshiping their false gods. He saw the temple crumble and catch fire. People disappeared in the flames.

"Those who cling to worthless idols forfeit the grace that could be theirs."

Once again Jonah saw the temple of the Lord, this time the place of sacrifice. He saw a priest coming toward a man with an offering for the altar. The chanting and singing grew louder. The golden light grew brighter.

"I, with a song of thanksgiving, will sacrifice to You. What I have vowed I will make good. Salvation comes from the Lord."

The man was Jonah himself. The scene grew brighter, mistier, but Jonah could see himself on his knees, ready to give his offering to the Lord. The next moment Jonah realized he was being thrown out of the great fish's mouth. He shot out of the water onto a sunny, sandy beach. His skin was bleached sickly pink and white. His clothes were pale rags. Seaweed covered him. God's voice spoke. Go to the great city of Nineveh and proclaim the message I give you."

Jonah did not speak. He simply got up and walked off to find the way to Nineveh.

Chapter Five – Preaching in Nineveh

Voices filled the air. Wagon wheels rumbled and creaked. Horses' hooves clattered. The noise was everywhere in the great city of Nineveh. On the busy streets, in the marketplace, in the houses of the city leaders, where the women got their water and washed their clothes -- a noisy, noisy city.

The city suddenly grew quiet. People heard a strange voice. They saw Jonah, still ragged and bleached from his trip by whale's stomach, walked all over the city, preaching. "Forty more days and Nineveh will be overthrown!"

"What is that fellow saying?" asked a man beside a well, laughing. "Nineveh will be overthrown!" giggled a woman, almost spilling her waterpot.

"Yes!" laughed her friend. "In forty days, he says!" She picked up her laundry basket as she watched Jonah pass. Jonah did not pay any attention to those who laughed. He went on, repeating his message.

"Who is he? Where did he come from?" asked a man in fine clothes outside the biggest temple in the city.

"He looks so horrible!" shuddered one of the wicked women who hung around outside the temple waiting for men.

"I'd say he's a Hebrew," said another man. "They have a powerful God, people say."

The woman beside him clung tightly to his arm. "People tell about that God punishing sins -- destroying people - judging them for disobeying Him."

Another man nodded. "That fellow looks like he's been judged for sin himself." "If that God is angry with us," cried a woman, "we are lost!"

In another part of the city, people gathered in the street. Some were laughing about Jonah. Some weren't sure what to think. Some were frightened. Suddenly the King of Nineveh himself appeared among them. Before they could bow to him, the king threw aside his royal robes. Underneath he wore old sack material, and he had ashes on his head. He sat down in the dusty street.

"I have heard about the prophet of the True God who has been reaching in our city," shouted the king. "God will destroy us if we do not repent. Do not let man or beast, herd or flock taste anything; do not let them eat or drink. Let man and beast be covered with sackcloth. Let everyone call with all his might upon God.

"Let them give up their evil and their violence. Who knows? God may yet relent and with compassion turn from His fierce anger so that we will not die."

Immediately the people went looking for sack clothing and ashes for themselves and their animals. In every part of the city people shouted and cried out to God for forgiveness. Some tore their clothes.

Many wept, threw dust into the air, or fell on the ground.

"God save us!" some cried. "Forgive us for our sins!" "We've been so wicked!"

"Don't destroy us, please!" "We repent!"

"God, help us!" "Have mercy on us!" "We're so sorry!"

Jonah could hear these many voices. He heard them as he climbed a hill outside Nineveh, faint and faraway. He had finished preaching and wanted to see what God would do. The hill was tall and barren. Jonah sat down, looking downhill. Dusty, dry weeds and dead trees surrounded him.

"O, Lord, isn't this what I said when I was back home? That's why I ran to Tarshish. I know You are a gracious and compassionate God, slow to anger and abounding in love, a God Who changes His mind about sending disasters. Now, O Lord, take away my life, for it is better for me to die than to live."

The voice of God spoke to Jonah. "Have you any right to be angry?"

Jonah got up and built a shelter of sticks. He sat inside. The sun beat down on him. Jonah grew hot. A gourd vine grew up over his shelter. The leaves spread out and blossoms appeared. Jonah relaxed and fell asleep. Night fell. God sent a worm to chew away the roots of the vine. The vine quickly curled up and died. The sun rose hot and bright. God sent a dry, whistling east wind. Jonah felt full of misery. He groaned. His body was covered with sweat. He thrashed and moaned. He grasped at the shreds of the vine and hugged them to him. The hot wind blew the hut down around him.

"I want to die!" gasped Jonah.

God's voice spoke again. "Do you have the right to be angry about the vine?"

"Of course I do!" snapped Jonah. "It gave me shade and comfort."

God said, "You have been concerned about a vine you did not water or make grow -- a thing that grew up and died in one night. Nineveh has 120 thousand people who can't tell their right hand from their left, and animals as well. Shouldn't I be concerned about all those lives? Shouldn't I save them?"

Epilogue – Dinner in Emmaus

Cleopas and Thaddeus were startled to realize that they had arrived at the house in Emmaus as the stranger finished talking. The storyteller started to go on his way, but the two friends told him he must stay and have dinner with them.

"What was it about Jonah that the Lord was trying to tell us?" Cleopas asked.

"Jonah preached repentance to his enemies-- people who wanted to kill him," Thaddeus said thoughtfully. Cleopas nodded.

"Jonah ran away, just like we did," Thaddeus said sadly.

"I don't think that's why the Lord talked about him, though," Cleopas frowned.

"No. It's that three days and three nights," Thaddeus insisted. "That's what He said. Three days in the whale's belly, three days in the heart of the earth."

"After three days in the whale's belly, Jonah got vomited up!" Cleopas joked.

"Ugh!" said Thaddeus. "What's that got to do with the Lord?"

"If He was the Son of God, how could He be dead? That's what I can't understand."

"He never sinned. Death is for sinners! But He was dead!"

"Come. It is time to give thanks," the stranger broke in as they sat down at the table. He prayed for the food and reached for the basket of bread.

"Three days and three nights -- and Jonah came out again. Three days and three nights -- and the Lord – will –"

Thaddeus reached out his hand for the bread the stranger held out to him. Suddenly both Cleopas and Thaddeus stared in amazement.

"It is the Lord!" They both shouted together. "He is alive!"

As quickly as they spoke the words, Jesus vanished.

"The Lord will come out! In three days, He will come out!" shouted Cleopas.

"Death cannot hold Him, any more than the whale could hold Jonah! Death has spewed Him out!"

"He is alive! Thaddeus! Thaddeus! We should have known it was Him. The way He taught the Scriptures -- "

"I know! It made my heart burn within me!"

"Mine too. I remember something else the Lord said."

"What? More about Jonah?"

"No. Not about Jonah. He told you at the Last Supper. 'Because I live, you shall live also.'"

"Because He lives, we shall live also! That's what He was trying to tell us. Believe, and live! Live forever!"

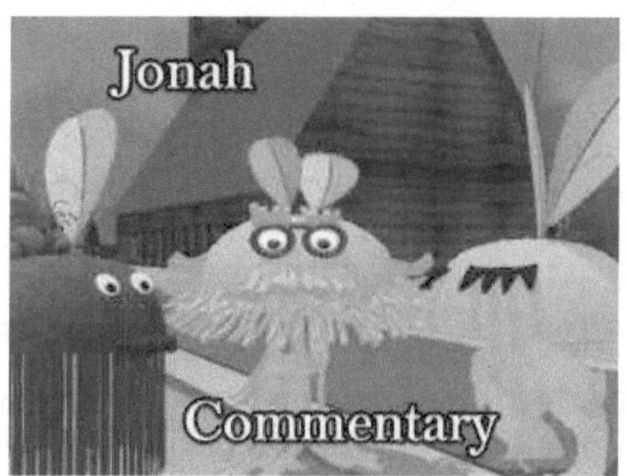

Jonah Commentary by the Anything Box Characters

Jerry: But most of the kids I know don't believe Jonah happened like that -- you know, the way the Bible says that it did.

Grampa: Probably more people choose not to believe Jonah than any other book in the Bible. It just seems too incredible to them. The book of Jonah is just one supernatural event after another. "Supernatural event" is just a fancy way of saying something happened that only God could do. The Bible calls that a Miracle. What these people do not want to admit is that they do not believe in God, at least, they do not believe in a god like the God of the Bible. They want a god they can control, someone who'll do whatever they want. They get mighty uncomfortable with a God that not only controls them but also controls everything around them. This is a God that will judge them someday, and they certainly don't want that. So they make up some sort of a god that they like, a god that gives them everything that they want.

Gloria: Jerry, even though they say they believe in God, their god isn't anything like the God of the Bible. But they still say they believe in the God of the Bible.

Grampa: Now that means they're calling God a liar. Oh, they would never say it like that, but, of course, that is exactly what they are doing. The way they would say it is something like, "Well, of course Jonah is true. You just have to understand what it is really saying. Now, that's just a sneaky way of saying Jonah isn't true. And if Jonah isn't true, then God is a liar. So when someone says something like, "You just have to understand what Jonah really means," or "Look for the higher meaning," or something else like that, what they are really doing is calling God a liar.

Jerry: No wonder the prophets got so angry with the people who called themselves God's children but they didn't live like they even knew God.

Grampa: Before you get too angry with them, remember that God says, "The heart is deceitful above all things." Most people do not even realize that they are calling God a liar. They think that they are helping out us poor old deluded literalists. They think there's something wrong with us for just believing what the Bible says.

Gloria: But God's still gonna judge them.

Grampa: That's right, Gloria. God's Word says that they are "without excuse." Why, the entire book of Jonah is filled with miracles to help us believe.

Jerry: There was a storm, and the great fish!

Grampa: Now, most people who do any reading at all know that some people today have been swallowed by whales and lived to tell about it. The real miracle of Jonah is that the great fish -- it might not even have been a whale, vomited Jonah up onto dry ground. People today who were swallowed by whales and lived to tell about it were cut out of the whale by other people. Maybe Jonah even died and God brought him back to life. We do not know for sure. The Bible just isn't clear about it. And what about the storm stopping as soon as the sailors threw Jonah overboard? Have you ever heard of a storm stopping just like that?

Jerry: Jesus made a storm stop just like this one did. Of course, people who don't believe Jonah don't believe Jesus either. I guess people don't repent just because they see something.

Grampa: What if they saw Jonah just after he came out of the great fish? After spending three days inside the stomach of a large fish, Jonah would look ... well ... not very good. Just looking at Jonah after that would make people think of the judgment of God.

Jonah: But the Bible doesn't say that.

Gloria: It doesn't say what the people of Nineveh thought of Jonah. Its seems that the only thing the Bible says is that Nineveh was "a city of three days' journey."

Grampa: People back then didn't explain things the way we do. The way they described Nineveh isn't the way we would describe it. That doesn't make them wrong. They just looked at things differently.

Jerry: But God didn't destroy Nineveh in forty days like Jonah said. That must mean the entire city repented. That's just not possible.

Grampa: If God had prepared the people, why do we have so much trouble believing that the entire city could repent? More people than the entire city of Nineveh have repented at one time in revivals in England, Germany, the United States and Canada. Some of the modern men of the people of God have been Martin Luther, John Calvin, Charles Spurgeon, Jonathan Edwards, and D. L. Moody. These have been but a few of the men of God used to bring large numbers of people to repentance. Why do some people have such a problem believing that Nineveh repented under Jonah's preaching?

Jerry: Same thing again. They just don't want to believe.

Grampa: Now the last major miracle that God gave to Jonah was his giant plant. Almost everyone has seen a plant wither and die in a matter of hours, so the plant's death was not a miracle. It was unusual, but not a miracle. But I have never heard of a large plant, large enough to shade a man, growing up in one night. The growth of that plant was a miracle of God.

Jerry: So that's the end of the story?

Grampa: If we are like the people of Nineveh, living in wickedness and sin, then the book of Jonah is a call for repentance. If we are believers in the One True God, then we have the call of Jonah to arise and preach. We must choose to either obey and follow Him, or be like Jonah and run away from the Lord.

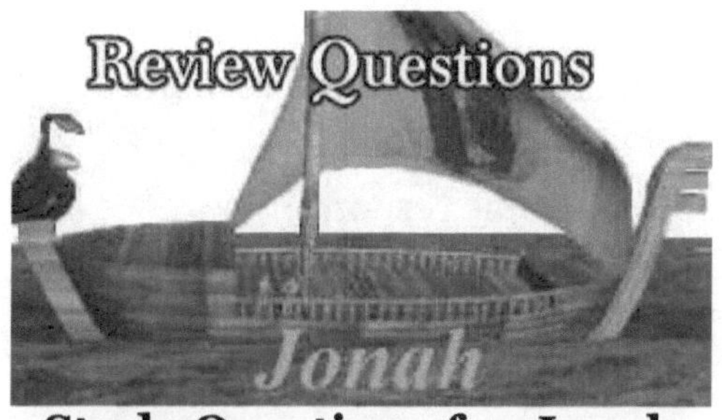

Study Questions for Jonah

1. Where was Jonah told to go to preach?
Nineveh

2. Why did he not want to go? (two reasons)
Afraid of enemies, wanted God to punish them

3. Where did he decide to go instead?
Tarshish

4. What happened on the ship Jonah took?
Deadly Storm

5. What did the sailors think would stop the trouble they were having?
Pray to their gods

6. What did Jonah tell them he had done?
Run from God

7. What did Jonah tell them to do?
throw him in the sea

8. How long was Jonah in the great fish?
3 days, 3 nights

9. What did Jonah think about while he was in the great fish? (Three things)
The temple worship, dying, God's salvation, obedience

10. How did Jonah get back on his way to Nineveh?
Fish spit him out on land

11. How many days did Jonah say Nineveh had left?
40

12. How did the King of Nineveh respond?
Told everyone to repent, fast, pray in sackloth

12. How did the people respond?
did as the king ordered

13. How did Jonah react?
Angry

14. Why did he go up on the hill?
see if the city would be destroyed

15. What did he say he wanted to do?
Die

16. What did God ask him?
Are you right to be angry?

17. What happened to make Jonah at first comfortable, then more miserable?
shade vine grew, then withered

18. What did God ask Jonah?
If Jonah cared about the vine, which he did nothing for, shouldn't God care about the Ninevites, people He made?

19. Why do more people choose to disbelieve Jonah than any other book in the Bible?
The miracles

20. What bothers people about believing in the God presented in the book of Jonah?
The idea of a God that controls them.

21. What are people doing by believing something else?
calling God a liar

22. What causes them to believe something different about God?
They want a God they can control

23. What is the real purpose of the miracles in Jonah?
help us believe

24. What is the difference between modern true stories about people being swallowed by whales and the case of Jonah?
The whale vomited Jonah up. Modern people were cut out.

25. What other case of a storm stopping instantly does Jerry bring up?
Jesus stopping the storm in Galilee

26. What modern incidents show that the repentance of the entire city of Nineveh is not impossible?
Historical revivals involving many thousands

27. What is the last miracle in Jonah?
The giant plant that grew, shaded Jonah and then suddenly died.

28. What two kinds of people need the messages of Jonah? How should each group respond to it?
Wicked, needing to repent, and believers, to rise and preach

The best gift you can give an author

is an honest, thoughtful review. Please consider leaving one online. Help us understand what you liked and didn't like about the book and why. Help authors reach more readers and spread your influence and ours. If you liked the book, please recommend it to your spouse, friends, pastors, teachers, cashiers, employers, – anybody and everybody you see each day. If you don't know what to say, remember Proverb 16:3 – Commit thy works unto the Lord and thy thoughts shall be established. Thank you!

OTHER BOOKS AND PRODUCTS FROM FINDLEY FAMILY VIDEO PUBLICATIONS

All our books (including Historical Fiction, SciFi, contemporary relationships short stories, and an Archaeological Mystery serial) are linked on our blog.

Elk Jerky for the Soul includes posts on current issues, excerpts from our fiction and nonfiction works, Bible teaching, travel and everyday observations, and more.

http://findleyfamilyvideopublications.com/

Visit our YouTube Channel

https://www.youtube.com/channel/UCGhwNpU115ARMwgYwTIJBrA/featured. Book trailers, video excerpts, project teasers, and more. Science, History, Literature, and biblical worldview studies are the focus of our book and video projects.

Historical Fiction

by Michael J. Findley

The Ephron the Hittite Series (Including boxed set of all titles)

Ephron Son of Zohar

Tawananna Daughter of Zohar

Heth Son of Canaan Son of Ham, Noah

Shelometh Daughter of Yovov Wife of Ephron

Zita Son of Ephron and Shelometh

Adult Romantic Suspense

by Mary C. Findley

The Men of the Realmlands series

Book One: The Baron's Ring

Book Two: The Captain's Blade

Send a White Rose

Chasing the Texas Wind

Carrie's Hired Hand (novella)

Young Adult Historical Adventure

by Mary C. Findley

Hope and the Knight of the Black Lion (plus illustrated version)

The Benny and the Bank Robber Series

Benny and the Bank Robber (Plus homeschool editions for student and teacher with review and vocabulary)

Doctor Dad

The Oregon Sentinel

Lines in Pleasant Places

Science Fiction and Fantasy

by Michael J. Findley

The Empire Saga (all six of the following books in one volume)

City on a Hill and Sojourner (Combined Novella and Short Story)

Nehemiah LLC (Full-length novel available as a standalone ebook, paperback, and hardcover versions)

Empire One: Humiliation

Empire Two: Repentance

Empire Three: Sanctification

Steampunk

by Sophronia Belle Lyon (pen name for Mary C. Findley)

The Alexander Legacy Steampunk Literary Tribute Series

Book One: A Dodge, a Twist, and a Tobacconist (including illustrated version)

Book Two: The Pinocchio Factor

Book Three: The Most Dangerous Game

Book Four: Beware the Bustle

Fantasy/Allegory

by Mary C. Findley

Allegorical clockwork novella inspired by Little Red Riding Hood

The Acolyte's Education

A Paranormal Urban Fantasy serial

His Sign: The Wait Is Over

His Sign 2: The Ezra Solution

Contemporary Fiction

by Mary C. Findley

Romantic Suspense Novella

Fall On Your Knees

Relationships Short Stories

Fifty Shades of Faithful

Fifty Shades of Faithful 2: In Living Color

The Great Thirst Serial Archaeological Mystery (including boxed set of all titles)

Part One: Prepared

Part Two: Purified

Part Three: Pursued

Part Four: Persecuted

Part Five: Persevering

Part Six: Protected

Part Seven: Prevailing

Murder Mystery

Mapped Out Murders

Nonfiction

by Mary C. Findley

*Write for the King of Glory, 2nd Edition (*updated, with tips on indie writing and publishing)

by Michael J. and Mary C. Findley

The Good, the Bad, and the Ugly: A Readers' and Writers' Guide for Believers

Biblical Studies (Teacher and student editions plus excerpts in *OT and NT Manuscript History)*

Antidisestablishmentarianism (illustrated and plain versions)

Serial versions, illustrated and plain

What Is an Establishment of Religion?

What Is Secular Humanism?

What Is Science?

What Are the Results of the Establishment of Secular Humanism?

The Conflict of the Ages series (All have teacher and student editions)

I. The Scientific History of Origins

II. The Origin of Evil in the World that Was

III. They Deliberately Forgot: The Flood and the Ice Age

IV. Ice Age Civilizations

V. The Ancient World

by Michael J. Findley

Short Recaps of longer nonfiction works (*Antidisestablishmentarianism* and *Conflict of the Ages)*

Disestablish: An Overview from Creation to the Ice Age

Under the Sun: The Truth about History from the Beginning

*****

www.ingramcontent.com/pod-product-compliance
Lightning Source LLC
LaVergne TN
LVHW041015150826
845672LV00001B/94

* 9 7 9 8 2 3 0 1 1 1 8 0 1 *